FRESH & EASY
Indian Vegetarian Cookbook

FRESH & EASY
Indian Vegetarian Cookbook

DELICIOUS RECIPES FOR EVERY DAY

MADE IN INDIA

Lustre Press
Roli Books

Published in India by Roli Books
M-75, Greater Kailash II Market
New Delhi-110 048, India
Ph: ++91-11-40682000
E-mail: info@rolibooks.com
Website: www.rolibooks.com

Cover design: Pallavi Agarwala
Editor: Priya Kapoor, Saachi Khurana
Layout design: Bhagirath Kumar

ISBN: 978-81-938608-3-0

CONTENTS

VEGETABLE AND FRUIT DISHES

PICKLES AND CHUTNEYS

BREADS, SIDES AND ACCOMPANIMENTS

INTRODUCTION

In a land so rich in cultural heritage, it is natural that Indian vegetarian cuisine is multifarious, delighting both the eye and the palate. Its many flavours and cooking traditions find their roots in its historical influences, from the Mughal era to the British Raj. The country's vast reservoir of spices, made from its abundance of tropical herbs, serves as garnishing and contains medicinal and preservative properties. Indeed, the range of Indian cuisine can amaze even a connoisseur.

India is the country with the highest reported rate of vegetarianism in the world, and this book fittingly pays homage to its myriad vegetarian dishes. It contains a mouth-watering selection of curries, rice and grain dishes, pickles, and other foods. Including over 70 easy-to-make recipes from all over the country, it showcases a flavourful blend of favourite Indian recipes along with several lesser-known delicacies. From Vazhakai Curry (sticky banana curry) to Yel Adai (coconut and rice pancakes) to Arbi Bonda (taro root fritters), it offers an incredible variety of dishes.

This book is a celebration of the diversity of Indian vegetarian cuisine. As India is a country that has a vast coastline and hosts six major climatic subtypes, it is no wonder that it is home to cuisines that use ingredients that are local and seasonal. There is a large world of Indian vegetarian cuisine that is still little-known both in India and abroad, and *Fresh & Easy Indian Vegetarian Cookbook* fills that gap.

CURRIES AND GRAVIES

SERVES 3

VAZHAKAI CURRY

Sticky banana curry

COOKING TIME
40 MINUTES

• Ingredients •

- 2 large or 3 medium-size unripe bananas, peeled
- 3 Tbsp (45 ml) vegetable oil
- ¼ tsp mustard (*rai*) seeds
- 1 tsp split black gram (*dhuli urad dal*)
- 1 dried red chilli (*sookhi lal mirch*)
- Pinch ground asafoetida (*hing*)
- ½ tsp ground turmeric (*haldi*)
- Salt, to taste

• Method •

1 Cook the bananas in a steamer or shallow vessel with enough water to cover until soft. Remove and dice into small pieces. Set aside.

2 In a small skillet over medium-high heat, heat the vegetable oil.

3 Add the mustard seeds. Cook until they begin to crackle.

4 Add the split black gram, dried red chilli, and asafoetida. Sauté until fragrant.

5 Add the diced bananas and turmeric. Season to taste with salt, cooking and stirring, until the mixture forms a sticky mass. Remove from the heat and serve hot.

SERVES 4–5

SHAHI PANEER

Cottage cheese in a rich gravy

COOKING TIME
20 MINUTES

• *Ingredients* •

- 2 lb, 3 oz (1 kg) cottage cheese (*paneer*) fingers
- ⅓ cup (80 ml) oil
- 6 cloves (*laung*)
- 2 bay leaves (*tej patta*)
- 3 cinnamon (*dalchini*) sticks
- 6 green cardamoms (*choti elaichi*)
- 1 cup (240 g) onion paste
- 2⅔ Tbsp (40 g) ginger (*adrak*) paste
- 2⅔ Tbsp (40 g) garlic (*lasan*) paste
- 2 tsp red chilli powder
- ¾ tsp turmeric (*haldi*) powder
- 1 tsp coriander (*dhaniya*) powder
- 2 tsp cashew (*kaju*) paste
- Salt, to taste
- ⅓ tsp red food colouring
- ¾ cup (180 g) yoghurt (*dahi*), whisked
- 2 tsp sugar
- ⅔ cup (160 ml) cream
- 1⅔ tsp garam masala
- ⅔ tsp green cardamom (*choti elaichi*) powder
- ⅔ tsp mace (*javitri*) powder
- 3 drops vetiver (*kewda*)
- Pinch saffron (*kesar*), dissolved in 1 Tbsp (15 ml) milk

• *Method* •

1 Heat the oil in a pan. Add cloves, bay leaves, cinnamon sticks and green cardamoms. Sauté over medium heat until they begin to crackle. Add the onion paste and stir-fry for 2–3 minutes.

2 Stir in the ginger and garlic pastes, red chilli powder, turmeric powder, coriander powder, cashew paste, salt and colouring. Add yoghurt, ½ cup warm water and sugar; bring to a slow boil and then simmer until the oil separates. Allow the curry to cool. Remove whole spices and blend to a smooth consistency.

3 Reheat the curry, stir in the cream, garam masala, cardamom powder, mace powder, vetiver and saffron mixture. Add the cottage cheese fingers and cook for another 5 minutes. Serve hot, garnished with chopped coriander, if desired.

SERVES 4

CHAKKA KURU MANGA CURRY

COOKING TIME
20 MINUTES

Jackfruit seeds and mango in a coconut curry

• Ingredients •

For the jackfruit-seed curry:

- 1 cup (150 g) jackfruit (*kathal*) seeds, skinned, halved lengthwise
- 4 green chillies, slit
- ½ tsp ground turmeric (*haldi*)
- Salt, to taste
- 3 baby onions
- Pinch cumin (*jeera*) seeds
- ½ tsp red chilli powder
- ½ cup (82.5 g) raw mango (*kairi*), sliced
- 1 cup (85 g) unsweetened coconut (*nariyal*), grated, dried
- 3 curry leaves (*kadhi patta*)

For the tempering:

- ¼ cup (60 ml) vegetable oil
- ½ tsp mustard (*rai*) seeds
- Pinch fenugreek seeds (*methi dana*)
- 3 Tbsp (30 g) onion, chopped
- 2 dried red chillies (*sookhi lal mirch*), quartered

• Method •

1 For the jackfruit-seed curry: In a medium-size saucepan, combine the jackfruit seeds with enough water to cover. Add the green chillies and turmeric. Season to taste with salt. Bring to a boil over high heat and cook for about 15 minutes until soft.

2 Meanwhile, in a blender or with a mortar and pestle, grind the baby onions, cumin seeds, and red chilli powder into a paste. When the jackfruit seeds are about three-fourths cooked (after about 10 minutes), add the mango and the onion-chilli paste. Mix well. Bring the mixture to a boil. Add the coconut and curry leaves. Cook until the gravy thickens.

3 For the tempering: In a skillet over low-medium heat, heat the vegetable oil. Add the mustard seeds, fenugreek seeds, onion, and dried red chillies. Sauté until the onion turns brown. Pour the tempering into the curry and mix well. Serve hot.

SERVES 4–5

PALAK PANEER

Spinach and cottage cheese curry

COOKING TIME
30 MINUTES

• Ingredients •

- 2 lb, 3 oz (1 kg) spinach (*palak*) leaves
- 1¼ cups (280 g) cottage cheese (*paneer*), cubed
- 10 cups (2.4 L) water
- Salt, to taste
- 4 tsp maize flour (*makkai*)
- 2 Tbsp (30 g) ghee
- 5 tsp onions, chopped
- 5 tsp ginger (*adrak*), finely cut
- 1 tsp red chilli powder
- 2 tsp tomato, finely cut
- 3 green chillies, chopped
- 2 tsp cream

• Method •

1 Remove the stalks of the spinach leaves. Wash and cut finely. Add water and salt; cook for 10 minutes. Drain the excess water and purée in a blender.

2 Add the cottage cheese cubes to the purée and mix well. Slowly stir in the maize flour and cook for 10 minutes. (This acts as a thickening agent.)

3 In a separate pan, heat the ghee. Brown the onions and most of the ginger. Add red chilli powder and stir. Pour this sauce over the spinach-cottage cheese mixture. Stir well and cook for 5 minutes.

4 Garnish with the remaining ginger, tomato pieces, green chillies and cream. Serve with a green salad and any bread of choice.

SERVES 4–6

MONJI KALIA

Kohlrabi in a spiced curd-based stew

COOKING TIME
30 MINUTES

• Ingredients •

- 1¼ cups (300 ml) vegetable oil, divided
- 2 lb, 3 oz (1 kg) kohlrabi (*ganth gobhi*), peeled, cut into 1-in. cubes
- 4 whole cloves (*laung*)
- 2 black cardamom (*badi elaichi*) pods, crushed
- Pinch ground asafoetida (*hing*)
- 1 cup (240 ml) water
- 1 Tbsp (7 g) ground aniseed (*saunf*)
- 1 tsp ground turmeric (*haldi*)
- 1 tsp ground dried ginger (*sonth*)
- ½ tsp garam masala
- Salt, to taste
- 2 Tbsp (30 g) yoghurt (*dahi*)
- 2 Tbsp (30 ml) milk
- 3 green cardamom (*choti elaichi*) pods

• Method •

1 In a skillet over low-medium heat, heat 1 cup of vegetable oil.

2 Add the kohlrabi and fry until golden. Transfer to paper towels to drain. Set aside.

3 In a deep pot over low-medium heat, heat 3 Tbsp of vegetable oil.

4 Add the cloves, black cardamom pods, and asafoetida. Sauté until fragrant.

5 Add the water and cover the pot to prevent the oil from spattering.

6 Carefully remove the lid and add the fried kohlrabi, aniseed powder, turmeric, ginger, and garam masala. Season to taste with salt. Increase the heat to medium and cook for 10 minutes.

7 In a small bowl, whisk the yoghurt and milk. Pour this into the pot. Stir continuously and bring to a boil. Cook for 5 minutes more and remove from heat.

8 In a small skillet over medium-high heat, heat the remaining 1 Tbsp of vegetable oil.

9 Add the green cardamom pods and sauté until they change colour. Remove and add to the stew pot. Serve hot.

SERVES 4–5

MUSHROOM, CAPSICUM AND CABBAGE CURRY

COOKING TIME
15 MINUTES

• Ingredients •

- 3 cups (300 g) mushrooms, quartered
- ¾ cup (120 g) cabbage (*bandh gobhi*), shredded
- 4 Tbsp (60 g) capsicums (*Shimla mirch*), julienned
- 4 red chillies, whole
- 1 tsp coriander (*dhaniya*) seeds
- ½ cup (120 ml) oil
- ½ cup (85 g) onions, sliced
- 4 tsp garlic (*lasan*) paste
- Salt, to taste
- 2 tsp garam masala
- 1 lb, 2 oz (500 g) tomatoes, chopped
- 4 green chillies, chopped
- 2 Tbsp (30 g) ginger (*adrak*), chopped
- 4 tsp green coriander (*hara dhaniya*), chopped

• Method •

1 Pound red chillies and coriander seeds with a pestle.

2 Heat 2 Tbsp oil in a wok. Stir-fry mushrooms over medium heat for a few minutes. Remove and keep aside.

3 In the same oil, stir-fry the cabbage until the liquid evaporates.

4 Heat the remaining oil in a wok. Sauté the onions till transparent. Add the garlic paste and stir for 20 seconds over medium heat.

5 Add the red chillies, coriander seeds, garam masala and salt. Stir for 30 seconds. Add tomatoes and cook till the oil separates from the mixture.

6 Stir in green chillies, ginger and half the green coriander. Add stir-fried mushrooms and cabbage; cook for a few minutes. Garnish with julienned capsicums and remaining green coriander. Serve hot.

SERVES 4

PAHARKAI PITLAI

Bitter gourd cooked with powdered spices

COOKING TIME
15 MINUTES

• Ingredients •

- 3–4 medium-size bitter gourds (*karela*), cut into thin circular or semicircular pieces
- ½ cup (100 g) split red gram (*masoor dal*), cooked
- 1 tamarind (*imli*), lemon-size
- 2 tsp refined oil
- 1 tsp mustard (*rai*) seeds
- ¼ tsp turmeric (*haldi*) powder
- Salt, to taste
- 2 Tbsp (10 g) coriander (*dhaniya*) seeds
- 2 Tbsp (25 g) split Bengal gram (*chana dal*)
- 4–5 black peppercorns (*sabut kali mirch*)
- 3–4 dried red chillies (*sookhi lal mirch*)
- Pinch asafoetida (*hing*)
- 1 cup (100 g) coconut (*nariyal*), scraped
- 4–5 curry leaves (*kadhi patta*)

• Method •

1 Soak the tamarind in a cup of hot water for 5 minutes and extract the juice.

2 Heat ¼ tsp oil; sauté the mustard seeds till they start spluttering. Add the vegetable, turmeric powder, salt, and tamarind extract. Cook till the vegetable is done, adding water if necessary.

3 Heat the remaining oil; sauté all the remaining ingredients except curry leaves and split red gram till the coconut is reddish brown. Remove; grind to a fine powder.

4 Add the cooked split red gram, curry leaves, and spice powder to the bitter gourd mixture. Stir and cook for 2 minutes. Add water, if required to get the correct consistency.

5 Serve with rice and fried *appalam* (poppadum).

SERVES 4–6

POOSHANIKKA MOR KUZHAMBU

COOKING TIME
20 MINUTES

Steamed pumpkin in yoghurt gravy

• Ingredients •

- 2½–2¾ cups (350–400 g) pumpkin (*kaddu*), peeled, cut into small cubes
- 2 cups (480 g) yoghurt (*dahi*), whipped
- Salt, to taste
- ¼ tsp turmeric (*haldi*) powder
- 1 tsp rice powder
- 1 tsp split red gram (*masoor dal*)
- 1 tsp split Bengal gram (*chana dal*)
- 1 tsp cumin (*jeera*) seeds
- 3 Tbsp (12 g) coconut (*nariyal*), grated
- 2 green chillies
- ½ tsp refined oil
- ¼ tsp mustard (*rai*) seeds
- 5–6 curry leaves (*kadhi patta*), pinched

• Method •

1 Steam the pumpkin with a little salt and water.

2 Mix the yoghurt with salt, turmeric powder, and rice powder.

3 Soak the split red gram, Bengal gram, and cumin seeds in warm water for 5 minutes. If the coconut isn't freshly grated, it should be soaked as well. Drain and grind all the ingredients along with the green chillies.

4 Mix this paste with the yoghurt mixture.

5 Add the yoghurt mixture to the cooked pumpkin and cook on low heat till it simmers. Remove.

6 Heat the oil in a small pan; add the mustard seeds and curry leaves. When the seeds start spluttering, remove and add to the pumpkin mixture.

SERVES 4–6

SURAKKA MOR KOOTTU

COOKING TIME
20 MINUTES

Bottle gourd in spiced yoghurt

• Ingredients •

- 1 medium-size bottle gourd (*ghia*), peeled, chopped into small pieces
- Salt, to taste
- 5 Tbsp (20 g) coconut (*nariyal*), grated
- 3 green chillies
- 1 tsp cumin (*jeera*) seeds
- 1 cup (240 g) yoghurt (*dahi*)
- 1 tsp rice powder
- ½ tsp refined oil
- ¼ tsp mustard (*rai*) seeds
- ½ tsp split black gram (*dhuli urad dal*)
- 4–5 curry leaves (*kadhi patta*), pinched

• Method •

1 Boil the bottle gourd in a little water and salt.

2 Grind the coconut, green chillies, and cumin seeds into a wet paste.

3 Mix the paste with the yoghurt. Add rice powder; mix well.

4 Add the above to the boiled bottle gourd and cook for 5 minutes.

5 Heat the oil in a small pan; add mustard seeds, split black gram, and curry leaves. When the seeds start spluttering, pour it onto the cooked mixture.

CHEF'S NOTE

This *mor koottu* can also be made with cabbage.

SERVES 4

PORITHA KOOTTU

Vegetables in green gram gravy

COOKING TIME
15 MINUTES

• Ingredients •

- ¼ cup (50 g) split green gram (*moong dal*)
- 3 cups (720 g) medium-size vegetables (potatoes, drumsticks, snake gourd, aubergines), chopped
- Salt, to taste
- 2–3 dried red chillies (*sookhi lal mirch*)
- ¼ tsp cumin (*jeera*) seeds
- 1½ Tbsp (6 g) coconut (*nariyal*), grated
- ½ tsp refined oil
- ¼ tsp mustard (*rai*) seeds
- ¼ tsp split black gram (*dhuli urad dal*)
- Pinch asafoetida (*hing*)
- 5 curry leaves (*kadhi patta*)

• Method •

1 Pressure cook the split green gram.

2 Boil the vegetables in 1 cup of salted water till tender. Remove and drain.

3 Grind together the dried red chillies, cumin seeds, and coconut into a paste.

4 Add the paste and the cooked split green gram to the cooked vegetables. Stir.

5 Heat the oil in a pan; add the mustard seeds, split black gram, asafoetida, and curry leaves. When the seeds start spluttering, add to the green gram mixture; stir well and remove from heat.

6 Serve hot with rice or roti.

SERVES 4–6

VATRAL KUZHAMBU

Dried vegetable gravy

COOKING TIME
20 MINUTES

• Ingredients •

- A handful medium-size vegetables (cluster beans, berries, aubergines, etc.), dried, salted
- 1 tamarind (*imli*), lemon-size, soaked in 1 cup (240 ml) water for 5 minutes
- 4–5 tsp refined oil
- ½ tsp mustard (*rai*) seeds
- ½ tsp fenugreek seeds (*methi dana*)
- ½ tsp split red gram (*masoor dal*)
- 2 dried red chillies (*sookhi lal mirch*)
- Pinch asafoetida (*hing*)
- 4–5 curry leaves (*kadhi patta*)
- 2½ tsp sambhar powder
- 1½ tsp salt to taste
- 1 tsp rice powder, dissolved in 2 tsp water

• Method •

1 Extract the tamarind juice.

2 Heat the oil in a cooking pan; add mustard seeds, fenugreek seeds, split red gram, dried red chillies, asafoetida, and curry leaves. When the seeds start spluttering, add the dried salted vegetables and sambhar powder. Continue frying till the mixture turns reddish in colour.

3 Add the tamarind extract, salt, and some more water to make up about 3 cups of gravy. Bring the mixture to a boil till it is reduced to 2 cups.

4 Add the rice powder and boil further for a minute. Remove and serve hot with steamed rice and roasted *appalam* (poppadum).

SERVES 4–6

KOTTU KUZHAMBU

Pumpkin and onion in tamarind gravy

COOKING TIME
20 MINUTES

• Ingredients •

- 1 tamarind (*imli*), lemon-size, soaked in 1 cup (240 ml) warm water for 5 minutes
- 2 medium-size onions, peeled, chopped
- 1¼ cup (250 g) red pumpkin (*lal kaddu*), peeled, chopped
- 4–5 tsp refined oil
- ½ tsp mustard (*rai*) seeds
- ½ tsp fenugreek seeds (*methi dana*)
- 2 dried red chillies (*sookhi lal mirch*)
- Pinch asafoetida (*hing*)
- 4–5 curry leaves (*kadhi patta*)
- 2½ tsp sambhar powder
- 1½ tsp salt to taste
- 1 tsp rice powder, dissolved in 2 tsp water

• Method •

1 Extract the tamarind juice.

2 Heat the oil in a pan; add the mustard seeds, fenugreek seeds, dried red chillies, asafoetida, and curry leaves. When the seeds start spluttering, add the onions and sauté till they change colour. Add the pumpkin and sambhar powder; cook till the pumpkin turns reddish in colour.

3 Add the tamarind extract, salt, and some more water to make about 3 cups of gravy. Bring the mixture to a boil till it is reduced to 2 cups.

4 Add the rice powder and mix well. Let it boil further for a minute and remove from heat.

SERVES 4

VENGAYA THIYAL

Onion gravy

COOKING TIME
15 MINUTES

• *Ingredients* •

- 1 tamarind (*imli*), lemon-size, soaked in 1 cup (240 ml) warm water
- 2 cups (250 g) onions, finely sliced
- 7 tsp refined oil
- 2 tsp coriander (*dhaniya*) seeds
- ½ tsp cumin (*jeera*) seeds
- 5 dried red chillies (*sookhi lal mirch*)
- ½ cup (40 g) coconut (*nariyal*), grated
- ¼ tsp turmeric (*haldi*) powder
- Salt, to taste
- ¼ tsp mustard (*rai*) seeds
- 5 curry leaves (*kadhi patta*)

• *Method* •

1 Extract the tamarind juice.

2 Heat 2 tsp oil in a pan; sauté the coriander seeds, cumin seeds, dried red chillies, and coconut till the mixture turns light brown. Remove and grind to a fine paste.

3 Heat 4 tsp oil in the same pan; sauté the onions till the colour changes. Add the ground spice paste, turmeric powder, salt, and tamarind extract; mix well. Add 3 cups of water and cook till the mixture thickens. Remove from heat.

4 Heat the remaining oil; add mustard seeds and curry leaves. When the seeds start spluttering, remove and add to the mixture.

5 Serve hot with steamed rice.

SERVES 4

ERISSERI

Elephant yam and plantain with fried coconut

COOKING TIME
15 MINUTES

• Ingredients •

- 1⁴⁄₅ cups (200 g) elephant yam, peeled, cut into cubes
- 2 medium-size plantains, peeled, cut into cubes
- ¼ tsp turmeric (*haldi*) powder
- 1½ tsp salt to taste
- ¾ cup (60 g) coconut (*nariyal*), grated
- 1 tsp black peppercorns (*sabut kali mirch*)
- 1 tsp cumin (*jeera*) seeds
- 3 Tbsp (45 ml) coconut oil
- ¼ tsp mustard (*rai*) seeds
- ¼ tsp split black gram (*dhuli urad dal*)
- 5 curry leaves (*kadhi patta*)

• Method •

1 Boil 1½ cups of water with turmeric powder and salt; add the vegetables (the yam first and the plantains after a few minutes; or cook the yam separately, drain and add to the plantains) and cook.

2 Grind ½ cup coconut, peppercorns, and cumin seeds into a fine paste; mix with the vegetables.

3 Heat 2 Tbsp coconut oil in a pan; add the mustard seeds, split black gram, and curry leaves. When the seeds start spluttering and the gram turns reddish, remove and add to the vegetables.

4 In the remaining coconut oil, fry the remaining coconut till it turns golden, and add to the vegetables. Stir for a few seconds. Serve hot.

SERVES 2–4

ALOO POTOL DALNA

Potato and parwar curry

COOKING TIME
15 MINUTES

• Ingredients •

- 6⅓ cups (700 g) potatoes, diced
- ⁴⁄₅ cup (200 g) parwars (*parwal*)
- ¾ cup (180 ml) mustard oil (*sarson ka tel*)
- 2 cloves (*laung*)
- 2 green cardamoms (*choti elaichi*)
- 1 cinnamon (*dalchini*) stick
- 1 bay leaf (*tej patta*)
- 5 black peppercorns (*sabut kali mirch*)
- 4 Tbsp (60 g) tomatoes, chopped
- Salt, to taste
- 1 tsp turmeric (*haldi*) powder
- ½ tsp red chilli powder
- 1 cup (240 ml) water

• Method •

1 Heat the mustard oil in a wok. Sauté the potatoes and parwars. Drain the excess oil and keep aside.

2 To the same oil, add the cloves, green cardamoms, cinnamon, bay leaf and black peppercorns. Sauté for a few seconds and then add the tomatoes. Cook for 2–3 minutes.

3 Add salt, turmeric powder, red chilli powder, potatoes and parwars. Stir for a few seconds.

4 Add the water and cook till the potatoes are done and the water is absorbed.

SERVES 4

STUFFED POTATOES IN FENUGREEK AND SPINACH CURRY

COOKING TIME
1 HOUR

• Ingredients •

- 2 lb, 3 oz (1 kg) round, medium-size potatoes
- 11 Tbsp (45 g) mint (*pudina*) leaves
- 5½ cups (90 g) green coriander (*hara dhaniya*)
- 10 green chillies, chopped
- ½ tsp cumin (*jeera*) seeds
- 1 tsp dried mango powder (*amchoor*)
- 4 tsp raisins (*kishmish*)
- Salt, to taste
- 6 Tbsp (90 ml) oil, for frying
- ½ tsp turmeric (*haldi*) powder
- ⅓ cup (80 g) tomatoes, chopped
- 13 cups (390 g) spinach (*palak*), chopped
- 1½ cups (90 g) fenugreek (*methi*) leaves, chopped
- 2 tsp red chilli powder
- 3 Tbsp (45 g) yoghurt (*dahi*)
- 1 tsp garam masala
- 1 tsp coriander (*dhaniya*) powder
- 2 Tbsp (30 g) ghee

• Method •

1 Peel and scoop out a spoonful from the centres of the potatoes; deep-fry the shells till they are crisp and golden brown.

2 Grind mint, green coriander, green chillies, cumin seeds, mango powder, raisins and salt with very little water to make a chutney and set aside.

3 Heat 6 Tbsp oil in a wok. Add turmeric powder, tomatoes, spinach and fenugreek leaves. Sauté lightly.

4 Stir in red chilli powder and salt and cook till the curry thickens. Mix in the yoghurt, garam masala, coriander powder and ghee.

5 Remove from heat and allow to cool. Blend to a thick purée and reheat.

6 Spoon the prepared chutney into the potatoes.

7 Place the potatoes in a shallow dish and pour the curry over them.

8 Serve hot.

CHEF'S NOTE

When mint leaves are available in plenty, dry them in the sun and add rock salt and cumin powder. Store in an airtight container and use whenever necessary.

SERVES 4

DUM ALOO KASHMIRI

COOKING TIME
25 MINUTES

Kashmiri-style, slow-cooked potatoes

• Ingredients •

- 8 medium-size potatoes
- ½ cup (120 ml) oil
- 1 tsp caraway seeds (*shahi jeera*)
- 1 tsp aniseed (*saunf*)
- 2 medium-size onions, chopped
- 1 tsp black cardamom (*badi elaichi*), pounded
- 5 Tbsp (75 g) raisins (*kishmish*)
- 8 Tbsp (75 g) cashews (*kaju*)
- Salt, to taste

For the curry:

- 6 Tbsp (60 g) onions, chopped
- 1¼ cups (300 g) yoghurt (*dahi*), whisked
- 1 cup (240 g) tomato purée
- 4 tsp ginger-garlic (*adrak-lasan*) paste
- 2¾ Tbsp (40 g) almond (*badam*) paste
- 1 tsp aniseed (*saunf*)
- ½ tsp mace (*javitri*) powder
- ½ tsp caraway seeds (*shahi jeera*)
- 4 green cardamoms (*choti elaichi*)
- 6 cloves (*laung*)
- 4 tsp red chilli paste
- 2 tsp cumin (*jeera*) powder
- 2.5 Tbsp (15 g) coriander (*dhaniya*) powder
- Salt, to taste
- Oil, for frying

• Method •

1 Peel potatoes, slice off the tops. Scoop out the centres. Fry the shells and centres to golden brown. Allow the centres to cool and mash.

2 Heat oil in a wok; sauté caraway seeds and aniseed. Add onions and sauté till transparent. Add the fried potato centres, cardamom powder, raisins and cashews. Stir-fry for a few minutes. Season with salt. Keep aside.

3 Stuff the fried shells with the prepared mixture and keep aside.

4 For the curry, heat oil in a thick-bottomed pan. Sauté onions till transparent. Add yoghurt, tomato purée, ginger-garlic paste, almond paste, aniseed, mace, caraway seeds, green cardamoms, cloves, red chilli paste, cumin powder, coriander powder and salt. Stir-fry for 8–10 minutes.

5 Place the stuffed potatoes in the curry; cover the lid and seal with dough. Cook on slow fire for 10 minutes. Remove from heat. Place the potatoes in a serving dish, strain the curry and pour on top of the potatoes.

6 Serve immediately, accompanied by any Indian bread of choice.

SERVES 4–5

VEGETABLE KORMA

COOKING TIME
20 MINUTES

Mixed vegetables in cashew / almond curry

• Ingredients •

- 1 cup (130 g) carrots (*gajar*), diced
- 1¼ cups (125 g) cauliflower (*phool gobhi*), cut into small florets
- ⅔ cup (120 g) French beans (*fransi bean*)
- ¾ cup (120 g) green peas (*hara mattar*)
- 1⅕ cups (120 g) mushrooms
- 1 cup (110 g) potatoes, diced
- ½ cup (85 g) onions, chopped
- 4 Tbsp (60 ml) oil
- 10 cashews / almonds (*kaju / badam*)
- 10 raisins (*kishmish*)
- 6 cloves (*laung*)
- 3 cinnamon (*dalchini*) sticks
- 1 bay leaf (*tej patta*)
- ¾ tsp cumin (*jeera*) seeds
- 8 green cardamoms (*choti elaichi*)
- 2⅔ Tbsp (40 g) ginger (*adrak*) paste
- 2⅔ Tbsp (40 g) garlic (*lasan*) paste
- 5 tsp green chilli paste
- ½ cup (120 g) cashew (*kaju*) paste
- 1 cup (240 g) yoghurt (*dahi*), whisked
- Salt, to taste
- ⅔ tsp white pepper (*safed mirch*) powder
- 4 Tbsp (60 g) cream
- 1 tsp ginger (*adrak*), julienned
- 3 tsp green coriander (*hara dhaniya*), chopped

• Method •

1 Heat a little oil in a pan. Lightly fry the cashews / almonds and the raisins. Keep aside.

2 Parboil all the vegetables.

3 Heat the remaining oil. Add the cloves, cinnamon sticks, bay leaf, cumin seeds and green cardamoms and sauté until golden. Grind to a paste.

4 Add the ginger and garlic pastes, green chilli paste, cashew paste and the ground spices; cook until the oil separates from the gravy.

5 Add the yoghurt and cook on low heat for 5 minutes.

6 Add the parboiled vegetables, salt and white pepper. Cover and cook on low heat for 5–6 minutes.

7 Add the cream and transfer to a serving bowl. Garnish with ginger juliennes, green coriander and the fried dry fruits.

CHEF'S NOTE

To keep button mushrooms fresh, put them into boiling water to which a pinch of salt has been added. Take them out after a minute, drain, cool and store in a plastic, airtight container.

SERVES 6

POTATO AND PANEER DUMPLINGS IN CURRY

COOKING TIME
1 HOUR

• Ingredients •

For the dumplings:

- 3–4 medium-size potatoes, boiled, mashed
- 1 lb, 2 oz (500 g) cottage cheese (*paneer*), grated
- 3 cups (48 g) green coriander (*hara dhaniya*), chopped
- (45 g) 3 Tbsp mixed nuts, finely chopped
- ½ tsp turmeric (*haldi*) powder
- Pinch asafoetida (*hing*) powder
- 1 Tbsp (15 g) ginger (*adrak*), finely shredded
- 1–2 green chillies, deseeded, finely chopped
- ½ tsp dried mango powder (*amchoor*)
- 1 tsp lemon (*nimbu*) juice
- 1½ tsp salt
- 2 Tbsp (15 g) cornflour
- Oil, for frying

For the curry:

- 2⅔ Tbsp (40 g) cashews / almonds (*kaju / badam*), finely chopped
- 1 Tbsp (15 g) ginger (*adrak*), finely chopped
- 2 green chillies, chopped
- 1½ tsp coriander (*dhaniya*) powder
- 1 tsp cumin (*jeera*) powder
- ½ tsp turmeric (*haldi*) powder
- 1 cup (240 ml) water
- 5 Tbsp (75 ml) ghee
- 1 tsp cumin (*jeera*) seeds
- 1 (1-in.) piece cinnamon (*dalchini*) stick
- 4 cloves (*laung*)
- 2½ cups (600 g) tomatoes, finely chopped
- Salt, to taste

• Method •

1 For the dumplings, knead the grated cottage cheese till smooth and creamy. Add mashed potatoes, coriander, nuts, turmeric powder, asafoetida powder, ginger, green chillies, dried mango powder, lemon juice, salt and cornflour. Knead and mix thoroughly.

2 Lightly oil your hands and divide the mixture into 12 portions. Roll each portion into a ball. Place all the balls on a tray lined with plastic wrap and set aside.

3 Heat oil in a wok till it starts smoking. Slide in a few balls at a time and fry until golden brown on all sides.

4 Remove, drain excess oil on a paper towel and keep aside.

5 For the curry, process together the nuts, ginger, green chillies, coriander, cumin and turmeric powders and enough water to make a smooth paste. Set aside.

6 Moderately heat the ghee in a heavy-bottomed pan. Stir-fry the cumin seeds, cinnamon stick and cloves for 10–15 seconds.

7 Stir in half the tomatoes and the prepared paste. Cook until the liquid from the tomatoes dries up and the oil separates.

8 Add the remaining tomatoes, water and salt. Cover the pan and simmer for 10–15 minutes or until the curry has thickened slightly.

9 Carefully slip in the dumplings and bring the curry to a boil.

10 Spoon out the dumplings into a serving dish. Pour the curry on top and garnish with green coriander and cream, if desired.

11 Serve hot, accompanied by any Indian bread of choice and green salad.

RICE, LENTIL AND GRAIN DISHES

SERVES 4

KEERAI MASIYAL

Mashed amaranth and green gram tempered with mustard seeds

COOKING TIME
15 MINUTES

• Ingredients •

For the amaranth:

- 1 cup (200 g) split green gram (*moong dal*)
- 2 cups (480 ml) water, divided
- Salt, to taste
- 2 bunches amaranth leaves, washed, finely chopped

For the tempering:

- 1 Tbsp (15 ml) vegetable oil
- ½ tsp mustard (*rai*) seeds
- 1 tsp split black gram (*dhuli urad dal*)
- 1 dried red chilli (*sookhi lal mirch*)
- 1 tsp cumin (*jeera*) seeds
- ¼ tsp ground asafoetida (*hing*)

• Method •

1 For the amaranth: In a pressure cooker over medium-high heat, combine the split green gram with 1½ cups of water. Lock the lid in place and cook for 3 whistles. Let the pressure release, remove the lid, drain, and set aside.

2 In a saucepan, combine the remaining ½ cup of water with salt to taste. Bring to a boil over high heat.

3 Add the amaranth leaves. Cook until soft. Drain and mash lightly.

4 Stir the boiled split green gram into the mashed amaranth leaves.

5 For the tempering: In a skillet over low-medium heat, heat the vegetable oil.

6 Add the mustard seeds. Cook until the seeds begin to crackle.

7 Add the split black gram, dried red chilli, cumin seeds, and asafoetida. Sauté until the black gram turns golden and crispy.

8 Mix the amaranth-split green gram mix with the tempering.

9 Serve hot.

MAKES 8

YEL ADAI

Coconut and rice pancakes

COOKING TIME
40 MINUTES

• *Ingredients* •

- 2 cups (480 ml) water
- 1¼ cups (300 g) jaggery (*gur*; unrefined cane sugar)
- 3 cups (240 g) fresh coconut (*nariyal*), grated
- ¾ cup (180 g) ghee, divided
- 1 lb, 2 oz (500 g) rice, washed, soaked for 10–15 minutes, drained
- Salt, to taste
- 1 tsp green cardamom (*choti elaichi*) seeds
- 4 banana leaves, cut into 4-in. squares

• *Method* •

1 To prepare the jaggery syrup, boil the water, add the jaggery, and stir well. Remove the scum from time to time. Cook until the syrup is reduced to a quarter.

2 Add the coconut and cook for 5–8 minutes more. Stir in the ghee, reserving about 2 Tbsp.

3 In a food processor or grinder, combine the rice with enough water to make a batter of pouring consistency. Add salt to taste and the green cardamom seeds.

4 Smear the remaining ghee over the banana leaves. Pour the rice batter over the banana leaves (should make 8 pancakes), spread on the jaggery mixture, and fold in the shape of an envelope.

5 In a steamer, steam them for 18–20 minutes. Serve hot or cold.

MAKES 8

PATHIRI

Rice flour pancakes

COOKING TIME
30 MINUTES

• Ingredients •

- 2 cups (320 g) rice flour
- ½ tsp ground cumin (*jeera*)
- ½ tsp red chilli powder
- Salt, to taste
- Water, for kneading
- 2 Tbsp (30 g) ghee

• Method •

1 In a pan over medium heat, dry-roast the rice flour, cumin, and red chilli powder for 4–5 minutes. Remove the pan from the heat. Add salt to taste and a little water and knead into a soft dough.

2 Divide the dough into 8 balls. Roll each out into thin discs.

3 In a frying pan on low-medium heat, place a disc flat. Add 1 tsp ghee and pan-fry the bread until slightly brown on both sides.

4 Repeat until all are done.

5 Serve hot, smeared with ghee and accompanied with any curry of your choice.

APPAM

MAKES 8

Lacy rice pancakes

COOKING TIME
30 MINUTES

• Ingredients •

- 2 cups (400 g) rice, uncooked
- 1 cup (200 g) rice, cooked
- 1 cup (80 g) fresh coconut (*nariyal*), grated
- 2 Tbsp (25 g) sugar
- Water, as needed
- ½ tsp yeast
- Salt, to taste
- Vegetable oil, for shallow-frying

• Method •

1 In a blender or food processor, combine the raw and cooked rice, coconut, and sugar. Grind together with enough water to make a pourable batter.

2 Add the yeast. Pulse to combine. Season to taste with salt. Transfer the batter to a bowl, cover, and leave the batter to ferment overnight at room temperature.

3 Heat a heavy-bottomed skillet over medium heat.

4 Rub the skillet with a little vegetable oil and pour in 2 Tbsp of batter. Tilt the vessel around until the batter coats it. Sprinkle in some oil, cover the skillet, and cook for 2 minutes, or until the base is golden and the top is soft and pale. Remove and repeat with the remaining batter (should make 8 appams).

5 Serve hot with *elumichapazham rasam*, *chettinad nandu rasam*, or *araitha sambhar* (page 94), if desired.

MAKES 4

IDIAPPAM

String hoppers

COOKING TIME
30 MINUTES

• *Ingredients* •

- 1 cup (240 ml) water
- Salt, to taste
- 1½ Tbsp (22.5 ml) vegetable oil
- 1 cup (160 g) rice flour

• *Method* •

1 In a small pot with a lid over high heat, combine the water, salt, and vegetable oil. Cover the pot and bring to a boil.

2 Reduce the heat to low and slowly stir in the rice flour, mixing continuously so the mixture is lump-free.

3 Remove from the heat. Knead the mixture. Working in batches, pass the dough through a vermicelli press, pressing it onto a clean kitchen cloth.

4 In a steamer, steam for 3 minutes, or until cooked.

5 Serve hot with *elumichapazham rasam*, *chettinad nandu rasam*, or *araitha sambhar* (page 94), if desired.

SERVES 2–4

ANARASA

Rice flour delicacy

COOKING TIME
1 HOUR

• Ingredients •

- 2 cups (320 g) rice flour, finely ground
- 1 cup (200 g) sugar
- 4 tsp lemon (*nimbu*) juice
- ½ cup sesame (*til*) seeds
- 1¼ cups (300 g) ghee

• Method •

1 In a medium-size bowl, combine the rice flour, sugar, and lemon juice.

2 Cover the mixture with a deep dish turned upside down. Set aside for 4–5 hours.

3 Using just a little water knead the mixture into a dough.

4 Sprinkle the sesame seeds on a flat dish.

5 Divide the dough into small lemon-size balls and roll over the sesame seeds. Press the balls to form flat rounds, about 5 in. in diameter.

6 On a griddle over medium-high heat, heat the ghee.

7 In batches, fry the rice rounds until they turn golden.

8 Keep spooning the ghee (from the pan) over the rounds, but do flip them.

9 Transfer with a slotted spoon to paper towels to drain.

SERVES 4–6

KANGUCHI PULAO

COOKING TIME
30 MINUTES

Morel mushrooms cooked with fragrant rice

• Ingredients •

- 5 Tbsp (75 g) ghee
- 5 Tbsp (45 g) almonds (*badam*), blanched
- 6 whole cloves (*laung*)
- 6 green cardamom (*choti elaichi*) pods
- 4 black cardamom (*badi elaichi*) pods, crushed
- 3 (1-in.) cinnamon (*dalchini*) sticks
- 3 bay leaves (*tej patta*)
- 1 cup (100 g) morel mushrooms (*gucchi*), slit lengthwise and rinsed
- Pinch ground asafoetida (*hing*)
- Salt, to taste
- 1½ cups (300 g) rice, rinsed, soaked in water, drained
- 3 cups (720 ml) water
- 1 tsp ground dried ginger (*sonth*)
- 2 pinches saffron (*kesar*) threads
- 1 tsp garam masala

• Method •

1 In a heavy-bottomed pot over medium-high heat, heat the ghee.

2 Add the almonds, cloves, green and black cardamom pods, cinnamon sticks, and bay leaves. Cook until the spices begin to crackle.

3 Add the mushrooms and asafoetida. Season to taste with salt. Sauté for 1 minute.

4 Add the rice and stir gently.

5 Pour in the water and bring to a boil.

6 Stir in the ginger.

7 In a cup or small bowl, mix the saffron threads with 2 tsp of hot water and crush with a spoon. Add to the rice mixture. Cover the pot and cook for 15 minutes.

8 When most of the water is absorbed, reduce the heat to low and cook until the rice is tender. Sprinkle with the garam masala just before serving.

SERVES 4–6

VEGETABLE BIRYANI

Rice cooked with spices and vegetables

COOKING TIME
25 MINUTES

• Ingredients •

- 2 cups (400 g) basmati rice
- 3 medium-size carrots (*gajar*), peeled, chopped
- 2 cups (200 g) beans, stringed, chopped
- 3 medium-size onions, chopped
- 1¼ cups (200 g) green peas (*hara mattar*), shelled
- 3 Tbsp (45 ml) refined oil
- ½ tsp turmeric (*haldi*) powder
- 3–4 green cardamoms (*choti elaichi*)
- 2 cloves (*laung*)
- 1 (1-in.) piece cinnamon (*dalchini*) stick
- 1 bay leaf (*tej patta*)
- ½ cup (32 g) mint (*pudina*) leaves
- ½ cup (120 g) yoghurt (*dahi*)
- Salt, to taste
- 1 cup (240 ml) coconut (*nariyal*) milk

For the masala:

- 1 Tbsp (4 g) mint leaves
- 3 medium-size onions, chopped
- 6 garlic cloves (*lasan*)
- 1 (4-in.) piece ginger (*adrak*)
- 3–4 dried red chillies (*sookhi lal mirch*)
- 2–3 green chillies
- 1 bunch green coriander (*hara dhaniya*)
- 1 Tbsp (6 g) aniseed (*saunf*)
- 1–2 medium-size tomatoes, roughly chopped

• Method •

1 For the masala: Grind all the ingredients mentioned into a paste.

2 Heat 1 Tbsp oil in a pan; fry the vegetables, adding turmeric powder. Keep aside.

3 Heat the remaining oil and sauté the green cardamom, cloves, cinnamon stick, and bay leaf for a few seconds.

4 Add the masala paste and fry till the oil floats on top. Add the mint leaves and yoghurt; stir.

5 When the mixture thickens, add salt, rice, coconut milk, and the required quantity of water to cook the rice.

6 When the rice is cooked, add the fried vegetables and mix well.

7 Serve with *pachadi*.

VEGETABLE AND FRUIT DISHES

SERVES 3–4

SURATI SALAD

Crunchy cucumber salad

COOKING TIME
5 MINUTES

• Ingredients •

- 1 tsp vegetable oil
- Pinch ground asafoetida (*hing*)
- 1 Tbsp (12.5 g) split Bengal gram (*chana dal*), roasted
- 1 Tbsp (9 g) peanuts, roasted, chopped
- 1 Tbsp (4 g) coconut (*nariyal*), fresh, grated
- 1 tsp sesame seeds (*til*), roasted
- 2 green chillies, finely chopped
- ½ tsp sugar
- Salt, to taste
- 1 cup (300 g) cucumber, small, diced

• Method •

1 In a skillet over medium-high heat, heat the vegetable oil.

2 Add the asafoetida and split Bengal gram. Sauté for 2 minutes.

3 In a large bowl, mix the peanuts, coconut, sesame seeds, green chillies, sugar, and salt.

4 Add the split Bengal gram-asafoetida mixture and cucumber. Taste to adjust the seasoning and serve.

ARBI BONDA

MAKES 6

Crispy taro root fritters

COOKING TIME
30 MINUTES

• Ingredients •

- 2 cups (450 g) boiled, mashed taro root (*arbi*)
- 6 green chillies, chopped
- 1 Tbsp (1 g) green coriander (*hara dhaniya*), finely chopped
- 1 Tbsp (15 g) yoghurt (*dahi*)
- 1 tsp fresh ginger (*adrak*), chopped, peeled
- Pinch ground asafoetida (*hing*)
- Salt, to taste
- 1 cup (125 g) all-purpose flour (*maida*)
- ½ cup (60 g) chickpea flour (*besan*)
- ½ cup (80 g) rice flour
- Pinch baking soda
- Water, as needed
- Vegetable oil, for frying

• Method •

1 In a medium-size bowl, stir together the mashed taro root, green chillies, green coriander, yoghurt, ginger, and asafoetida. Season to taste with salt. Shape the mixture into medium-size balls.

2 In another medium-size bowl, stir together the flours, baking soda, and enough water to make a semi-thick batter.

3 In a wok over medium heat, heat the vegetable oil for frying.

4 Working in small batches, dip the taro root balls into the batter and then carefully lower them into the hot oil.

5 Cook until crisp. With a slotted spoon, transfer to paper towels to drain.

6 Serve hot with mint-coriander chutney, if desired.

SERVES 4–6

URULAIKIZHANGHU PALIYA

COOKING TIME
20 MINUTES

Potatoes in onion-tomato masala

• Ingredients •

- 1 lb, 2 oz (500 g) medium-size potatoes, unpeeled
- 1½ cups (360 ml) water, plus more for cooking the potatoes
- 2 Tbsp (30 ml) vegetable oil
- ½ tsp mustard (*rai*) seeds
- 1 dried red chilli (*sookhi lal mirch*)
- 1 (1-in.) piece fresh ginger (*adrak*), peeled, finely chopped
- 1 green chilli, slit
- 1 medium-size onion, finely chopped
- 1 medium-size tomato, diced
- ¼ tsp ground turmeric (*haldi*)
- Pinch ground asafoetida (*hing*)
- Salt, to taste
- Juice of 1–2 lemons (*nimbu*)
- 1 small bunch green coriander leaves (*hara dhaniya*), finely chopped

• Method •

1 In a pressure cooker over medium heat, combine the potatoes with enough water to cover. Lock the lid and cook for 3 whistles. Let the pressure release and remove the lid. When cool enough to handle, peel the potatoes and cut them into chunks. Set aside.

2 In a skillet over medium-high heat, heat the vegetable oil. Add the mustard seeds. Sauté until the seeds begin to crackle.

3 Add the dried red chilli, ginger, green chilli, and onion. Sauté until the onions turn light brown.

4 Add the tomato and turmeric. Sauté for 2 minutes.

5 Add the water, asafoetida, and season to taste with salt. Cover the skillet and reduce the heat to low. Simmer the mixture for 5 minutes.

6 Add the potatoes. Stir to combine and cook for 3 minutes more. Remove the skillet from the heat and set aside to cool a bit.

7 Add the lemon juice and serve garnished with green coriander.

SERVES 6

KOOTU THEEYAL

An aromatic vegetarian delicacy from Kerala

COOKING TIME
20 MINUTES

• Ingredients •

- ¼ cup (60 ml) coconut oil, divided
- 12 dried red chillies (*sookhi lal mirch*), divided
- 1 cup (85 g) unsweetened coconut (*nariyal*), grated, dried
- ¾ tsp fenugreek seeds (*methi dana*)
- 3 cups (910 g) okra (*bhindi*), diced
- 3 cups (250 g) aubergine (*baigan*), diced
- 3 cups (405 g) cucumber, diced
- 3 cups (330 g) potato, diced
- ½ cup (85 g) Madras onion (pearl onion), slit, cut into small slices
- ½ tsp mustard (*rai*) seeds
- 2 medium-size onions, sliced
- 1 lemon-size tamarind (*imli*), dissolved in 2 cups (480 ml) water, strained
- Salt, to taste

• Method •

1 In a wok over low-medium heat, heat 1 tsp of coconut oil.

2 Add 8 dried red chillies, the coconut, and fenugreek seeds. Sauté until the coconut turns brown. Remove from the heat. Set aside to cool.

3 Transfer the fried ingredients to a food processor or mortar and pestle. Add a little water and grind them into a fine paste.

4 Return the wok to the heat and add 3 Tbsp of coconut oil.

5 Add the okra, aubergine, cucumber, potato, and pearl onions. Cook until the vegetables are tender. Remove the vegetables and set aside.

6 In the same wok, add the remaining 2 tsp of coconut oil.

7 When hot, add the mustard seeds. Sauté until the seeds begin to crackle.

8 Add the sliced onions and the remaining 4 dried red chillies. Cook until the onions turn brown.

9 Add the okra, aubergine, cucumber, potato, and pearl onions back to the wok. Stir well to combine.

10 Mix in the tamarind extract and spice paste. Season to taste with salt. Cook until the mixture is heated through. Remove from the heat and serve hot.

SERVES 3–4

VAREKA UPERI

Stir-fried raw banana with black-eyed peas flavoured with coconut and curry leaves

COOKING TIME
35 MINUTES

• Ingredients •

- ¼ cup (50 g) black-eyed peas (*lobia*)
- 2 green chillies
- 4 garlic (*lasan*) cloves
- ½ tsp ground turmeric (*haldi*)
- Pinch cumin (*jeera*) seeds
- 1½ cups (120 g) unsweetened coconut (nariyal), grated, dried
- 2 raw medium-size bananas, sliced
- 2 Tbsp (30 ml) vegetable oil
- 1 tsp mustard (*rai*) seeds
- 2 dried red chillies (*sookhi lal mirch*), quartered
- 1 Tbsp (10 g) Madras onion (pearl onion), finely chopped
- 3 curry leaves (*kadhi patta*)
- Salt, to taste

• Method •

1 In a pressure cooker over medium-high heat, combine the black-eyed peas with enough water to cover. Lock the lid and cook for 3 whistles or until the peas are cooked. Let the pressure release, drain the peas, transfer to a saucepan, and set aside to cool.

2 In a blender or with a mortar and pestle, grind the green chillies, garlic, turmeric, and cumin seeds into a paste.

3 Add the coconut and grind again until smooth.

4 Stir the bananas into the black-eyed peas.

5 Add the coconut-spice paste in the centre. Cover the pan and cook for about 3 minutes. Uncover and mix well once before removing from the heat.

6 In a skillet over medium-high heat, heat the vegetable oil.

7 Add the mustard seeds, dried red chillies, baby onion, and curry leaves. Sauté until the seeds begin to crackle and the leaves turn brown. Add the black-eyed pea mixture and stir well. Season to taste with salt. Remove from the heat and transfer to a serving dish.

SERVES 6

BATTER-COATED STUFFED TOMATOES

COOKING TIME
30–40 MINUTES

• Ingredients •

- 3–4 medium-size tomatoes, whole
- $\frac{3}{5}$ cup (140 g) cottage cheese (*paneer*)
- ¼ tsp black pepper (*kali mirch*), ground
- ¼ tsp asafoetida (*hing*) powder
- 2 cups (32 g) green coriander (*hara dhaniya*), chopped
- Oil, for frying

For the batter:

- 8 Tbsp (60 g) chickpea flour (*besan*), sifted
- ¼ tsp cayenne pepper (*Kashmiri lal mirch*)
- ¼ tsp salt
- ¼ tsp baking powder
- ¼ cup (60 ml) water, cold

• Method •

1 Slice stems off the tomatoes and hollow out the centres; drain upside down on a paper towel.

2 Knead cottage cheese and spices together. Fill each tomato cup with the mixture.

3 Mix the ingredients for the batter, adding water slowly. Whisk until the batter is smooth and thick enough to seal in the filling and to evenly coat the tomatoes.

4 Dip each filled tomato in the batter, coating evenly. Deep-fry until golden brown on all sides. Remove and drain on paper towels. Serve hot.

SERVES 4

STIR-FRIED MUSHROOMS

COOKING TIME
20 MINUTES

• Ingredients •

- 1 lb, 2 oz (500 g) mushrooms
- 4½ tsp oil
- 2 medium-size onions, sliced
- 1 tsp garlic (*lasan*) paste
- 1 medium-size tomato, chopped
- ½ tsp turmeric (*haldi*) powder
- ½ tsp garam masala
- ½ tsp red chilli powder
- Salt, to taste
- 1 cup (16 g) green coriander (*hara dhaniya*), chopped

• Method •

1 Cut mushrooms into slices.

2 Heat oil and fry onions until golden in colour. Add garlic paste and chopped tomato; mix well.

3 Put in turmeric powder, garam masala, chilli powder and salt and fry for 3–4 minutes. Stir in mushrooms and simmer until the mushrooms are tender, adding very little water if necessary.

4 Garnish with coriander and serve hot.

SERVES 4–5

BEANS PORIYAL

Beans with split black gram

COOKING TIME
20 MINUTES

• Ingredients •

- 2 lb, 3 oz (1 kg) beans
- ½ tsp turmeric (*haldi*) powder
- 1 tsp salt
- 4 Tbsp (60 ml) oil
- 1 tsp mustard (*rai*) seeds
- 1 tsp split black gram (*dhuli urad dal*)
- 2 red chillies, whole
- 2 medium-size onions, chopped
- 2 green chillies, chopped
- Salt, to taste
- ½ medium-size coconut (*nariyal*), fresh, grated

• Method •

1 Remove the strings from the beans and chop finely.

2 Boil the beans in 1 cup of water, adding turmeric powder and salt. Cook until the beans are almost done. Drain excess water and keep aside.

3 Heat oil in a wok. Add mustard seeds, split black gram and whole red chillies. When mustard seeds begin to crackle, add chopped onions and green chillies.

4 Stir-fry for 4–5 minutes.

5 Add beans and stir-fry till beans are cooked.

6 Add salt to taste and the grated coconut; stir and remove from fire.

7 Serve immediately, accompanied by a curry dish and steamed rice or parathas.

SERVES 4–5

ALOO PALAK

Ginger-flavoured potatoes in spinach cream

COOKING TIME
25 MINUTES

• Ingredients •

- 2¼ cups (250 g) potatoes, cubed, boiled
- 2 lb, 3 oz (1 kg) spinach (*palak*)
- 10 (2.4 L) cups water
- Salt, to taste
- 2 tsp maize flour (*makkai*)
- 2 Tbsp (30 g) ghee
- 5 tsp onions, chopped
- 5 tsp ginger (*adrak*), chopped fine
- 1 tsp red chilli powder or 3 green chillies, chopped
- 2 tsp cream

• Method •

1 Remove the stalks of the spinach leaves. Wash and chop finely. Add water and salt and cook for about 10 minutes. Drain the water and purée the spinach.

2 Add the potato cubes to the purée and mix well.

3 Gradually stir in the maize flour and cook for 10 minutes. (This acts as a thickening agent.)

4 In a separate pan, heat the ghee and brown the onions and half the ginger. Add the red chilli powder / green chillies and sauté for a minute.

5 Pour this over the potato-spinach mixture, stir well and heat through. Serve, garnished with ginger juliennes and cream, accompanied by a dal, green salad and any Indian bread of choice.

SERVES 4–5

BAGHAR-E-BAIGAN

Aubergines tempered with fenugreek and garlic

COOKING TIME
20 MINUTES

• *Ingredients* •

- 1 lb, 2 oz (500 g) medium-size aubergines (*baigan*), whole
- 3⅓ Tbsp (52.5 g) tamarind (*imli*)
- 1 cup 3 Tbsp (200 g) onions, chopped
- 2 Tbsp (30 g) ginger (*adrak*) paste
- 2 Tbsp (30 g) garlic (*lasan*) paste
- 3 tsp sesame seeds (*til*)
- 3 tsp coconut (*nariyal*), slivered, desiccated
- 3 tsp red chilli powder
- 3 tsp coriander (*dhaniya*) powder
- 1 cup (240 ml) oil
- 3 curry leaves (*kadhi patta*)
- 2 tsp cumin (*jeera*) powder
- ¼ tsp fenugreek seeds (*methi dana*)
- 2 Tbsp (30 g) garlic (*lasan*) cloves, chopped
- 1 tsp turmeric (*haldi*) powder
- Salt, to taste

• *Method* •

1 Soak the tamarind in warm water and squeeze out the pulp.

2 Quarter all the aubergines without disjoining them from the stem. Grind the onions with the ginger and garlic pastes to a fine mixture.

3 Roast the sesame seeds, coconut, chilli powder and coriander powder. Add 1 Tbsp water and grind to a fine paste.

4 Heat the oil in a pan; add the curry leaves, cumin, fenugreek and garlic cloves and sauté for the *baghar* (tempering).

5 Add the ground spices, aubergines, tamarind pulp, turmeric powder, salt and ½ cup of water to the *baghar* and cook on a low fire till the aubergines become tender. Serve with steamed rice.

CHEF'S NOTE

To remove the skin from garlic cloves easily, slice the cloves half down the convex side. The peels will come off easily. If you chop garlic with a little salt, it will not stick to the knife or the chopping board.

SERVES 4–5

ALOO GOBHI SUKHI

Peppy potatoes and spicy cauliflower

COOKING TIME
40 MINUTES

• Ingredients •

- 1 lb, 2 oz (500 g) medium-size potatoes, cut into quarters
- 1 lb, 2 oz (500 g) cauliflower (*phool gobhi*), cut into small pieces
- ⅓ cup (80 ml) oil
- 2 bay leaves (*tej patta*)
- 5 green cardamoms (*choti elaichi*)
- 5 red chillies, whole, cut into half
- 1⅓ tsp cumin (*jeera*) seeds
- ½ cup (85 g) onions, chopped
- 2⅔ Tbsp (40 g) ginger (*adrak*) paste
- 2⅔ Tbsp (40 g) garlic (*lasan*) paste
- 1 tsp turmeric (*haldi*) powder
- 1⅔ tsp red chilli powder
- 2 tsp coriander (*dhaniya*) powder
- 1 cup (240 g) tomatoes, chopped
- Salt for seasoning
- 5 black peppers (*kali mirch*)
- 3 tsp garam masala
- 1 cup (16 g) green coriander (*hara dhaniya*), chopped
- 2 tsp ginger (*adrak*), julienned

• Method •

1 Heat the oil in a pan. Add the bay leaves, cardamoms, whole red chillies and cumin seeds. Sauté over medium heat.

2 Add the chopped onions, ginger and garlic pastes, turmeric powder, red chilli powder and coriander powder; sauté for 45–60 seconds. Add tomatoes and cook for another 5 minutes.

3 Add the cauliflower and potatoes and cook over medium heat for 10 minutes. Add 1 cup of water, cover and cook for 10 minutes on low heat. Season with salt, black pepper and garam masala and stir.

4 Serve, garnished with green coriander and ginger juliennes, as an accompaniment to any Indian bread of choice.

CHEF'S NOTE

Take small, tender cucumbers, slit them lengthwise and remove the seeds. Put the cucumbers in a plastic bag and chill them. Just before serving, fill up the hollow spaces with chopped raw vegetables. You can now serve cucumber boats on the table.

SERVES 4–5

SPICED CAULIFLOWER

Delicious fried and baked cauliflower

COOKING TIME
45 MINUTES

• Ingredients •

- 5 cauliflowers (*phool gobhi*), small, whole, destemmed
- Oil, for frying
- 1 cup (170 g) onions, chopped
- ½ cup (70 g) cashews (*kaju*)
- 6 green cardamoms (*choti elaichi*)
- 1 tsp turmeric (*haldi*) powder
- 2 tsp red chilli powder
- 5 tsp ginger (*adrak*) paste
- 5 tsp garlic (*lasan*) paste
- 2 tsp garam masala
- 1 cup (240 g) yoghurt (*dahi*), whisked
- Salt, to taste
- 2 Tbsp (30 g) butter
- 1 Tbsp (15 ml) lemon (*nimbu*) juice
- ½ tsp mace (*javitri*) powder

• Method •

1 Wash and clean the cauliflowers.

2 Heat oil in a wok and deep-fry each cauliflower over medium heat until almost cooked.

3 In the same oil, fry onions and cashews (saving a few for garnishing). Grind to a fine paste.

4 Heat 5 Tbsp oil in a pan. Add cardamoms and sauté for a few seconds. Add turmeric powder, red chilli powder, ginger and garlic pastes and garam masala and cook for 30 seconds.

5 Add onion-cashew paste and whisked yoghurt. Cook for 10 minutes on low heat and season with salt.

6 Arrange the fried cauliflower in a baking dish and pour the curry over each cauliflower. Bake in a moderate oven of 175°C (350°F) for 10 minutes.

7 Garnish with fried cashews, melted butter, lemon juice and mace powder. Serve hot.

SERVES 4

URULAIKIZHANGU MASALA

Spicy potatoes

COOKING TIME
20 MINUTES

• Ingredients •

- 6 medium-size potatoes, boiled, peeled, chopped into small pieces
- 1–2 Tbsp (15–30 ml) refined oil
- 1 tsp split black gram (*dhuli urad dal*)
- 1 tsp split Bengal gram (*chana dal*)
- 2 dried red chillies (*sookhi lal mirch*)
- 5–6 curry leaves (*kadhi patta*)
- Pinch asafoetida (*hing*)
- 2 medium-size onions, finely chopped
- 1 (1-in.) piece ginger (*adrak*), finely chopped
- 4 green chillies, finely chopped
- 1 tsp chickpea flour (*besan*)
- ¼ tsp turmeric (*haldi*) powder
- Salt, to taste
- Juice of 2 lemons (*nimbu*)

• Method •

1 Heat the oil in a pan; sauté the black and Bengal grams, dried red chillies, half of the curry leaves, and asafoetida till the split black gram turns a golden brown.

2 Stir in the onions, ginger, green chillies, and the remaining curry leaves. Fry till the onions change colour.

3 Mix the chickpea flour and turmeric powder in a cup of water and pour it into the pan. Add the potatoes and stir in the salt. Add water to form sufficient gravy. Lower heat and simmer for 5 minutes or till the gravy thickens.

4 Remove from heat and mix in lemon juice.

5 Serve hot with puri.

SERVES 4–6

POTATO BASKETS

Potatoes stuffed with chickpeas and spices

COOKING TIME
20 MINUTES

• Ingredients •

- 8 large potatoes, boiled, peeled
- ¾ cup (150 g) chickpeas (*kabuli chana*), boiled
- 1 Tbsp (10 g) chaat masala
- 1 Tbsp (15 g) ginger (*adrak*), finely chopped
- 2 tsp green chillies, finely chopped
- 1 cup (16 g) green coriander (*hara dhaniya*), finely chopped
- 2 Tbsp (30 ml) lemon (*nimbu*) juice
- Salt, to taste

• Method •

1 Cut the potatoes in half and carefully scoop out the centres.

2 Mix together the boiled chickpeas, chaat masala, chopped ginger, green chillies, green coriander, lemon juice and salt.

3 Put the mixture into the centre of the scooped potatoes. Arrange on a flat dish and serve.

SERVES 4–5

ALOO KI TARKARI

Spiced potato creoles

COOKING TIME
4–5 MINUTES

• Ingredients •

- 8 cups (880 g) potatoes, boiled, cubed
- ⅓ cup (80 ml) oil
- 5 red chillies, cut into half
- 1 tsp mustard (*rai*) seeds
- ½ cup (85 g) onions, chopped
- 4 tsp garlic (*lasan*), chopped
- 4 tsp ginger (*adrak*), chopped
- 2 tsp red chilli powder
- 1 tsp turmeric (*haldi*) powder
- 1⅔ tsp coriander (*dhaniya*) powder
- Salt for seasoning
- 1¼ cups (300 g) tomatoes, skinned, chopped
- 2 tsp green chillies, chopped
- 1 Tbsp (15 ml) lemon (*nimbu*) juice
- 4 tsp butter

• Method •

1 Heat the oil in a pan and sauté the red chillies and mustard seeds over medium heat.

2 Add the chopped onions, garlic and ginger; sauté over high heat for 5–6 minutes. Add the red chilli, turmeric and coriander powders; add salt and stir.

3 Add the chopped tomatoes and simmer on low heat until the oil separates from the gravy.

4 Add the boiled potato cubes, green chillies, lemon juice and salt; stir and cook for 5 minutes.

5 Melt the butter and pour over the potatoes before serving. Garnish with green coriander, if desired.

SERVES 4

BHARWAN KARELAS

Stuffed bitter gourds

COOKING TIME
45 MINUTES

• Ingredients •

- 2 lb, 3 oz (1 kg) medium-size bitter gourds (*karela*)
- Mustard oil (*sarson ka tel*) for frying
- ¼ cup (60 g) ghee
- Pinch asafoetida (*hing*) powder
- ½ cup (120 g) yoghurt (*dahi*)
- Salt, to taste
- 1 tsp red chilli powder
- 1 tsp ginger (*adrak*) paste
- ¼ cup (60 g) onion paste
- 2 tsp garlic (*lasan*) paste
- 2 tsp ginger (*adrak*), chopped
- 2 tsp green chillies, chopped
- 1 tsp green coriander (*hara dhaniya*), chopped
- ½ cup (120 ml) water

For the filling:

- 2 tsp sugar
- 2 tsp salt
- 1 cup (110 g) potatoes, boiled, cut into ½-in. cubes
- ½ tsp cumin (*jeera*)
- ½ cup (100 g) Bengal gram (*chana dal*), boiled, drained
- 2 tsp tamarind (*imli*) pulp
- 2 tsp fennel (*saunf*)
- 1 tsp red chilli powder
- 3 Tbsp (45 ml) mustard oil (*sarson ka tel*)

• Method •

1 Scrape the bitter gourds and boil them in water till half cooked. Slit, remove seeds and squeeze them gently to remove water. Heat mustard oil in a wok; deep-fry the bitter gourds till crisp. Keep aside.

2 Heat ghee in a pan. Add asafoetida with all the other ingredients.

3 Stir-fry for a few minutes, add water and cook till the water evaporates. Remove from heat. Stuff the bitter gourds with the ingredients for the filling (leave aside the mustard oil) and tie with a thread.

4 In a separate pan, heat 3 Tbsp mustard oil; add all the other ingredients along with the bitter gourds and cook till moisture evaporates. Remove and serve hot.

SERVES 4

BHARWAN SHIMLA MIRCH

Stuffed capsicums

COOKING TIME
45 MINUTES

• Ingredients •

- 3 medium-size capsicums (*Shimla mirch*)
- 4 Tbsp (60 ml) oil
- 1 Tbsp (15 g) ginger (*adrak*), chopped
- 2 tsp cumin (*jeera*) seeds
- ½ cup (55 g) potatoes, boiled, diced
- ½ cup (112.5 g) cottage cheese (*paneer*), cubed
- 2 Tbsp (16 g) red chilli powder
- 2 tsp turmeric (*haldi*) powder
- 1 tsp garam masala
- 2 Tbsp (14 g) cumin (*jeera*) powder
- 5 Tbsp (45 g) cashews (*kaju*)
- 5 tsp raisins (*kishmish*)
- 1 Tbsp (9 g) green chillies, chopped
- 1 cup (16 g) green coriander (*hara dhaniya*), chopped
- Salt, to taste

For the marinade:

- 1 cup (240 g) yoghurt (*dahi*), hung
- 4 tsp red chilli paste
- 4 tsp ginger-garlic (*adrak-lasan*) paste
- ½ tsp garam masala
- Salt, to taste
- Butter for basting
- ½ tsp cumin (*jeera*) powder

• Method •

1 Remove tops of capsicums and keep aside. Scoop out the seeds from the capsicum cups.

2 Heat oil in a wok. Add ginger and cumin seeds; sauté till they crackle. Add potatoes and cottage cheese. Sauté for a few minutes. Stir in dry spices along with the remaining ingredients. Mix well and remove from wok.

3 Fill the capsicums with this mixture and cover with the tops. For the marinade, mix all the ingredients and coat the capsicums with it.

4 Skewer the capsicums and cook in a tandoor / oven / grill for 10 minutes. Remove, baste with butter and cook further for 2–5 minutes. Serve hot.

SERVES 4–6

CRUNCHY OKRA

Spiced, fried okra

COOKING TIME
30 MINUTES

• Ingredients •

- 1 lb, 2 oz (500 g) okra (*bhindi*)
- Salt, to taste
- 1 tsp red chilli powder
- 1 tsp garam masala
- ½ tsp dried mango powder (*amchoor*)
- ½ tsp chaat masala
- 6 Tbsp (45 g) chickpea flour (*besan*)
- Oil, for frying
- 1½ tsp ginger (*adrak*), julienned
- 2 green chillies, sliced (optional)

• Method •

1 Snip off both ends of each okra and cut lengthwise into four slices.

2 Spread the slices on a flat dish; sprinkle evenly with salt, red chilli powder, garam masala, mango powder and chaat masala. Mix gently to coat okra evenly.

3 Sprinkle chickpea flour over the okra slices and mix to coat evenly, preferably without adding any water.

4 Divide the okra into two portions. Heat oil in a wok or a pan till it starts smoking. Fry one portion of coated okra slices, separating each lightly with a fork. Do not allow the slices to stick to each other.

5 Remove when both sides are crisp and brown in colour. Fry the other portion in the same way.

6 Garnish with julienned ginger and green chillies and serve at once.

SERVES 4

BAJJI

Vegetable fritters

COOKING TIME
10 MINUTES

• *Ingredients* •

- 2 cups (480 g) medium-size vegetables of choice (potatoes, onions, aubergines, and plantains), thinly sliced
- Refined oil, for frying

For the batter:

- 1 cup (120 g) chickpea flour (*besan*)
- ½ cup (80 g) rice flour
- ½ tsp red chilli powder
- Salt, to taste
- Pinch asafoetida (*hing*)
- 1 Tbsp (15 g) yoghurt (*dahi*)

• *Method* •

1 For the batter: Mix all the ingredients into a thick batter with some water.

2 Heat the oil in a wok; dip each vegetable slice in the batter and deep-fry till golden. Remove and drain the excess oil on paper towels.

3 Serve hot.

SERVES 4

KOS KARI

Cabbage tempered with mustard seeds

COOKING TIME
15 MINUTES

• *Ingredients* •

- 1 medium-size cabbage (*bandh gobhi*), chopped
- 1 tsp refined oil
- ½ tsp mustard (*rai*) seeds
- 1 tsp split black gram (*dhuli urad dal*)
- 2 dried red chillies (*sookhi lal mirch*)
- Salt, to taste
- 2 Tbsp (8 g) coconut (*nariyal*), grated (optional)

• *Method* •

1 Heat the oil in a pan; sauté the mustard seeds, black gram, and dried red chillies. When the seeds start spluttering, add the cabbage and salt; let it cook in its own juice if it is fresh, or add water. Cook covered.

2 When the cabbage is done, add the coconut and mix.

CHEF'S NOTE

You can cook beans in the same way.

SERVES 4–6

AVIAL

Mixed vegetables

COOKING TIME
15 MINUTES

• Ingredients •

- 1–2 medium-size carrots (*gajar*), chopped into small pieces
- ⅔ cup (100 g) green peas (*hara mattar*), shelled
- 2 medium-size potatoes, peeled, chopped into small pieces
- 2 drumsticks (*saijan ki phalli*), chopped into small pieces
- 1½ cups (200 g) white pumpkin (*petha*), peeled, chopped into small pieces
- 2 medium-size plantains, peeled, chopped into pieces
- 2 tsp salt, to taste
- 8 Tbsp (30 g) coconut (*nariyal*), scraped
- 4–5 green chillies
- 1 tsp cumin (*jeera*) seeds
- 1 tsp rice powder
- 1 cup (240 g) yoghurt (*dahi*)
- 3 Tbsp (45 ml) coconut oil
- ¼ tsp mustard (*rai*) seeds
- 4–5 curry leaves (*kadhi patta*), pinched

• Method •

1 Steam cook all the vegetables with salt. Remove and drain excess water.

2 Grind the coconut, green chillies, and cumin seeds with a little water into a smooth paste.

3 Mix this paste and the rice powder with the yoghurt. Mix the yoghurt mixture with the steamed vegetables. Cook for a few minutes.

4 Heat the coconut oil in a pan; sauté the mustard seeds and curry leaves. Remove and pour into the vegetable mixture. Mix and serve hot.

SERVES 2–4

ALOO CHORCHORI

Potato delight

COOKING TIME
30 MINUTES

• Ingredients •

- 1⅓ (200 g) potatoes, thinly sliced
- ⅘ cup (100 g) onions, thinly sliced
- 2 Tbsp (30 ml) oil
- 1 tsp turmeric (*haldi*) powder
- Salt, to taste
- 2 tsp red chilli powder
- ½ cup (120 ml) water

• Method •

1 Heat the oil in a wok; add the onions and sauté till light pink in colour.

2 Add the potatoes and sauté for 3–4 minutes.

3 Add the turmeric powder, salt, red chilli powder and water.

4 Cook over a medium flame till the potatoes are done and the liquid absorbed. Serve hot.

SERVES 2–4

ALOO BHATA

Mustard-flavoured mashed potatoes

COOKING TIME
5 MINUTES

• Ingredients •

- 2 medium-size potatoes, whole, boiled
- Salt, to taste
- 2 tsp green chillies, chopped
- 1 Tbsp (15 ml) mustard oil (*sarson ka tel*)

• Method •

1 Peel the potatoes while still hot.

2 Mash the potatoes; add salt, green chillies and mustard oil.

3 Take the potato mixture and shape into small balls. Serve with steamed rice.

CHEF'S NOTE

Cut potato chips will not stick to each other and turn out crisper when fried, if immersed in ice cold water for five minutes.

SERVES 4–5

DUM KE BAIGAN

Aubergines cooked on a slow fire

COOKING TIME
45 MINUTES

• Ingredients •

- 20 small, oval / round aubergines (*baigan*)
- ½ cup (120 ml) oil
- 12 red chillies, whole
- 2 tsp cumin (*jeera*) seeds
- 1⅓ tsp black pepper (*kali mirch*)
- 10 green cardamoms (*choti elaichi*)
- 5 cinnamon (*dalchini*) sticks
- 1 bay leaf (*tej patta*)
- 10 cloves (*laung*)
- 4 Tbsp (60 ml) malt vinegar (*sirka*)
- ¾ cup (180 g) onion paste
- 2⅔ Tbsp (40 g) ginger (*adrak*) paste
- 1 tsp turmeric (*haldi*) powder
- 2⅔ Tbsp (40 g) garlic (*lasan*) paste
- Salt, to taste
- 3 tsp green coriander (*hara dhaniya*), chopped

• Method •

1 Trim the stems of the aubergines. Slit open each aubergine crosswise, without disjoining it from the stem.

2 In a pan, heat 1 Tbsp oil over medium heat. Add the red chillies, cumin seeds, black pepper, green cardamoms, cinnamon sticks, bay leaf, and cloves; sauté over medium heat for 5–6 minutes. Cool and grind to a fine powder.

3 Mix in vinegar to make a fine paste.

4 Heat a little oil in a pan. Fry the aubergines, a few at a time, for 5–6 minutes or until they are half cooked. Remove from the heat and keep aside.

5 In the same pan, heat the remaining oil, add the onion paste and sauté over medium heat until the paste is lightly coloured.

6 Add the ginger and garlic pastes, turmeric powder and the ground spice paste. Stir and cook over medium heat for 4–5 minutes.

7 Add salt and ⅔ cup of hot water. Cook until the water evaporates and the oil separates from the sauce.

8 Arrange the fried aubergines in the sauce. Stir very carefully, cover and cook over a low flame or in a slow oven (*dum*) for 3–4 minutes. Garnish with green coriander.

CHEF'S NOTE

Peel onions under running water to avoid tears, or cut them into halves and soak them in water for a few minutes before cutting them. To skin small onions, soak them in boiling water for half a minute. Drain and cool; the skins will come off easily.

PICKLES AND CHUTNEYS

MAKES 2 CUPS

VARDENENGA ACHAR

Aubergine pickle

COOKING TIME
30 MINUTES

• Ingredients •

- 1¼ cups (300 ml) vinegar (*sirka*), divided
- 40 dried red chillies (*sookhi lal mirch*), skins only (stems and seeds discarded or saved for another use)
- 4½ Tbsp (68 g) minced garlic (*lasan*)
- ¾ tsp mustard (*rai*) seeds
- ¾ tsp fenugreek seeds (*methi dana*)
- ¾ tsp cumin (*jeera*) seeds
- 2 cups (164 g) 2-in. fingers aubergine (*baigan*), immersed in salted water
- Salt, to taste
- 1 cup (240 ml) sesame oil
- 3 Tbsp (45 g) fresh ginger (*adrak*), sliced, peeled
- 3 Tbsp (45 g) garlic (*lasan*), sliced
- 2 sprigs curry leaves (*kadhi patta*), leaves removed
- ¼ cup (50 g) sugar

• Method •

1 In a blender or food processor, combine ¼ cup of vinegar, the dried red chilli skins, garlic, mustard seeds, fenugreek seeds, and cumin seeds. Blend into a paste. Set aside.

2 Drain the aubergine and rub the pieces with salt. Set in the sun to dry for 4–5 hours.

3 In a skillet over medium heat, heat the sesame oil.

4 Add the ginger and garlic. Sauté until golden brown. With a slotted spoon, remove from the skillet and set aside.

5 Return the skillet to the heat and add the curry leaves, red chilli-spice paste, sugar, and remaining 1 cup of vinegar. Mix well.

6 Add the aubergine. Reduce the heat to low and simmer until the aubergine is tender.

7 Stir in the fried garlic and ginger. Season to taste with salt.

8 Store in a bottle in the refrigerator for up to two weeks.

MAKES 2½ CUPS

MOOLA KO ACHAR

Radish pickle

COOKING TIME
20 MINUTES

• Ingredients •

- 1 lb, 2 oz (500 g) radish (*mooli*), peeled, washed
- 3½ oz (100 g) red mustard seeds (*lal rai*)
- 4 tsp cumin (*jeera*) seeds
- ½ tsp *timmur* (a local variety of pepper; optional)
- 4 tsp red chilli powder
- 2 tsp ground turmeric (*haldi*)
- Salt, to taste
- 2 cups (480 ml) mustard oil (*sarson ka tel*), divided
- 2 tsp lemon (*nimbu*) juice

• Method •

1 Pat dry the radish and cut into 3-in. long pieces. Cut each piece diagonally into four. Replace if the radish has a white tinge.

2 Spread the radish out on a plate and sun-dry for 5–6 hours.

3 Using a grinder or mortar and pestle, coarsely grind the red mustard seeds, cumin seeds, and *timmur* (if using) together.

4 Combine the prepared ground ingredients, red chilli powder, and turmeric on another plate. Season to taste with salt.

5 Add 2–3 Tbsp (30–45 ml) mustard oil and lemon juice. Stir well to combine.

6 Add the radish pieces and toss well to coat the spice mix.

7 In a dry glass jar, put in the radish slices in batches. Press down after each addition to pack them well. Cover and put out in the sun for 2 days.

8 On the third day, shake the jar well. There should be water in it. Add the remaining mustard oil and store. The pickle is ready to serve in 6–7 days.

MAKES 2¼ CUPS

GOLBHENDA KO PAKAEKO

Tomato relish

COOKING TIME
30 MINUTES

• Ingredients •

- 4 Tbsp (60 ml) mustard oil (*sarson ka tel*)
- ½ tsp fenugreek seeds (*methi dana*)
- 2 dried red chillies (*sookhi lal mirch*), halved, seeded
- 2 tsp garlic (*lasan*), chopped
- 2 tsp ginger (*adrak*), shredded
- 1 lb, 2 oz (500 g) tomatoes, chopped
- ½ tsp ground turmeric (*huldi*)
- Salt, to taste
- 1 tsp cumin (*jeera*) seeds
- ¼ tsp red chilli powder

• Method •

1 In a skillet over medium-high heat, heat the mustard oil.

2 Add the fenugreek seeds and dried red chillies. Cook until the seeds begin to crackle.

3 Add the garlic and ginger. Cook for 2 minutes, or until the garlic turns brown.

4 Stir in the tomatoes and turmeric, and season to taste with salt. Stirring continuously, cook until the liquid gets absorbed.

5 Add the cumin seeds and red chilli powder. Cook, stirring continuously till the liquid dries and the oil begins to pull away from the sides of the dish.

6 Transfer to a dish and let it cool. This can be refrigerated for up to one week.

MAKES 2¼ CUPS

MARCHA NU ATHANU

Green chilli pickle

COOKING TIME
15 MINUTES

• Ingredients •

- 1 lb, 2 oz (500 g) green chillies, thick, washed, dried

For the filling:

- ¾ cup (204 g) Indian black salt (*kala namak*)
- ¾ tsp ground mustard (*rai*)
- ½ tsp ground asafoetida (*hing*)
- 1 tsp ground turmeric (*haldi*)
- 2 Tbsp (30 ml) vegetable oil
- Juice of 2 lemons (*nimbu*)

• Method •

1 In a medium-size bowl, slit each chilli lengthwise. Gently tap the sides to remove the excess seeds.

2 For the filling: In a small bowl, combine the black salt, mustard, asafoetida, turmeric, and the vegetable oil. Mix well.

3 Stuff the filling in each chilli. Preserve the stuffed chillies in a sterilized container. Top with leftover filling, if any.

4 Add the lemon juice and shake the container well.

5 Set aside for at least 1 day before serving.

SERVES 4

SESAME SEED AND TOMATO CHUTNEY

COOKING TIME
20 MINUTES

• Ingredients •

- 1 cup (240 g) tomatoes, chopped
- 2 Tbsp (30 g) sesame (*til*) seeds
- 2 Tbsp (30 ml) peanut oil
- 1 cup (170 g) onions, chopped
- ½ tsp red chilli powder
- ½ tsp turmeric (*haldi*) powder
- Pinch asafoetida (*hing*) powder
- 4 tsp black gram (*urad dal*), roasted

For the tempering:
- 2 Tbsp (30 ml) oil
- 5 red chillies, whole
- 2 tsp curry leaves (*kadhi patta*)
- ½ tsp mustard (*rai*) seeds

• Method •

1 Heat peanut oil in a pan. Add onions and sauté till light brown.

2 Stir in red chilli powder, turmeric powder, asafoetida powder and sesame seeds. Stir-fry for a few minutes.

3 Add tomatoes along with black gram and cook further for 10 minutes.

4 Remove from heat and allow to cool. Blend to make a paste and put in a bowl.

5 For the tempering, heat oil in a pan and add red chillies, curry leaves and mustard seeds. Sauté till they crackle and remove from heat.

6 Add the prepared tempering to the paste and serve.

MAKES 2½ CUPS

MIXED PICKLE

Pickle of cauliflower, turnips, and carrots

COOKING TIME
20 MINUTES

• Ingredients •

- 1 medium-size cauliflower (*phool gobhi*)
- 2–3 medium-size turnips
- 3 medium-size carrots (*gajar*)
- 1⅓ cups (320 ml) mustard oil (*sarson ka tel*)
- ½ cup (120 g) onions, puréed
- ¼ cup (60 g) ginger-garlic (*adrak-lasan*) paste
- 1 cup (200 g) sugar
- 1 cup (240 ml) vinegar (*sirka*)
- 5 tsp garam masala
- 4 tsp red chilli powder
- 4 tsp cumin (*jeera*) seeds
- 4 tsp mustard (*rai*) seeds
- Salt, to taste

• Method •

1 Cut the cauliflower into florets, and the turnips and carrots into thin slices. Dry in the sun for two days.

2 Heat mustard oil in a wok. Add onion purée and ginger-garlic paste and stir-fry for a few minutes.

3 Dissolve sugar in vinegar and keep aside.

4 Stir in the dry spices along with salt to taste and the vegetables. Cover and cook for 5–10 minutes.

5 Add the vinegar mixture to the vegetables and mix well. Remove from heat and allow to cool.

6 Transfer into a glass jar and cover with a cloth. Keep in the sun for 5 days. Serve as an accompaniment with any meal.

SERVES 4

VENGAYA TUKHAIYAL

Onion chutney

COOKING TIME
5 MINUTES

• *Ingredients* •

- 2 cups (350 g) onions, peeled, cut into quarters
- 7 tsp refined oil
- 5–6 dried red chillies (*sookhi lal mirch*)
- 1 tsp mustard (*rai*) seeds
- 3 tsp split black gram (*dhuli urad dal*)
- Pinch asafoetida (*hing*)
- 1 tamarind (*imli*), lemon-size
- 2 tsp salt

• *Method* •

1 Heat 3 tsp oil in a pan; fry the onions till the colour changes. Remove and keep aside.

2 Heat the remaining oil in the same pan; sauté the dried red chillies, mustard seeds, split black gram, and asafoetida till the mixture turns red in colour.

3 Remove and grind all the above with salt and tamarind. If desired, you can grind the onions, tamarind, salt, and dried red chillies first and then add the split black gram and mustard seeds for a final light grind. This way the chutney will have a crunchiness.

SERVES 4–5

ACHARI PANEER

Pickled cottage cheese preserve

COOKING TIME
15 MINUTES

• Ingredients •

- 2 lb, 3 oz (1 kg) cottage cheese (*paneer*), cubed
- ½ cup (120 ml) mustard oil (*sarson ka tel*)
- 10 cloves (*laung*)
- 10 green cardamoms (*choti elaichi*)
- 1½ tsp mustard (*rai*) seeds
- 1⅔ tsp fenugreek seeds (*methi dana*)
- 16 red chillies, whole
- 1 tsp caraway seeds (*shahi jeera*)
- 1 cup (170 g) onions, finely chopped
- 4 Tbsp (60 g) ginger (*adrak*) paste
- 4 Tbsp (60 g) garlic (*lasan*) paste
- 2 tsp red chilli powder
- 2 tsp turmeric (*haldi*) powder
- Pinch asafoetida (*hing*)
- 1½ cups (360 g) yoghurt (*dahi*), whisked
- Salt, to taste
- 1⅓ tsp black pepper (*kali mirch*), crushed
- 2 tsp sugar
- 6 garlic (*lasan*) cloves
- 4 tsp lemon (*nimbu*) juice
- 2 tsp green coriander (*hara dhaniya*), chopped

• Method •

1 Heat the oil in a pan. When it starts smoking, add the cloves, cardamoms, mustard seeds, fenugreek seeds, whole red chillies and caraway seeds; stir.

2 Add the chopped onions and sauté over medium heat until brown.

3 Add the ginger and garlic pastes, red chilli powder, turmeric powder and asafoetida. Stir and cook for 3–4 minutes. Add the yoghurt, bring to a boil and simmer over low heat until the oil separates from the gravy.

4 Add the cottage cheese cubes, salt, pepper, sugar, garlic cloves and lemon juice; stir and cook for one minute.

5 Transfer to a serving dish and garnish with green coriander.

CHEF'S NOTE

This dish can be stored in a sterilized bottle in the refrigerator for 5–7 days without the green coriander.

BREADS, SIDES AND ACCOMPANIMENTS

MAKES 2 CUPS

PERADA

Sweet guava cheese, most commonly eaten after a meal

COOKING TIME
40 MINUTES

• Ingredients •

- 6 medium-size guavas, peeled
- 1¼ cups (300 ml) water, divided
- Granulated sugar, as needed
- 1–2 tsp lemon (*nimbu*) juice
- 1 tsp butter (optional)
- Few drops red food colouring (optional)

• Method •

1 In a medium-size bowl, cut the guavas into pieces and scoop out the seeds.

2 Place a saucepan over medium-high heat. Add ¼ cup water and the scooped-out seeds. Boil for 3 minutes. Strain through a sieve. Reserve the liquid and discard the seeds.

3 In a pan over medium-high heat, heat the remaining 1 cup of water. Add the guava pieces and the reserved liquid. Cook until the guava becomes soft and pulpy. Set aside to cool.

4 In a blender or food processor, blend the mixture until smooth. Weigh the pulp.

5 Return the pulp to the pan. Add the sugar (which should be half the weight of the guava pulp). Cook, stirring continuously, until the mixture begins to leave the sides of the pan and is of soft-ball consistency. Add the lemon juice, butter, and red food colouring (if using). Stir well. Remove from the heat.

6 Pour the mixture on to a greased rimmed plate and spread evenly with the back of a greased spoon. Set aside to cool. Cut into diamond shapes to serve, or store in an airtight container for 10–14 days.

MAKES 7

MALABAR PAROTTA

Crisp pan-fried layered paratha

COOKING TIME
30 MINUTES

• Ingredients •

- ¾ cup (94 g) all-purpose flour (*maida*)
- 1 tsp baking powder
- 6 Tbsp (90 g) ghee, divided, plus more as needed
- Salt, to taste
- Water, as needed

• Method •

1 Sift the flour and baking powder together into a small bowl.

2 Add 1½ Tbsp of ghee and rub it into the flour mixture until well incorporated. Season to taste with salt and add enough water (about ¾ cup) to form a soft dough.

3 Knead well. Divide the dough into 7 portions. Roll each portion into a thin paratha and, using the remaining 4½ Tbsp of ghee, smear some over the surface of each. Roll each paratha from one end to the other and form it into a coil. Set aside for 15 minutes.

4 Roll the coils again into thin parathas.

5 Heat a griddle over low heat. Place the paratha on the griddle and cook for about 3 minutes. Turn it over and smear some ghee over and around it. Flip it again and do the same on the other side. Pan-fry until both sides are golden brown. Remove and repeat with all the parathas. Serve hot.

SERVES 4

BAMBAISON

Cardamom-flavoured milk sweet

COOKING TIME
1 HOUR

• Ingredients •

- 8 Tbsp (120 g) ghee, plus more to grease the plate
- 2 lb, 3 oz (1 kg) whole-milk fudge (*khoya*), grated
- 1¼ cups (250 g) sugar
- ½ cup (120 ml) milk
- 1 tsp ground green cardamom (*choti elaichi*)

• Method •

1 In a heavy-bottomed skillet over medium heat, heat the ghee.

2 Add the *khoya* and cook, stirring continuously, until light golden.

3 Add the sugar and milk; continue stirring until the sugar dissolves. Cook until the *khoya* becomes a lumpy mass and begins to pull away from the sides of the pan.

4 Remove from heat and mix in the green cardamom. Grease a flat plate with ghee and transfer the mixture to the plate. Spread it out with a greased spatula or the back of a serving spoon. Cut into pieces while the mixture is still hot. Remove from the plate only when it cools, and serve.

MAKES 8

SANNA

Steamed Goan rice bread

COOKING TIME
30 MINUTES

• *Ingredients* •

- 1 cup (200 g) rice, rinsed, soaked in water overnight, or for 8 hours, drained
- ½ cup (100 g) uncooked rice, rinsed, soaked in water overnight, or for 8 hours, drained
- ½ cup (42.5 g) unsweetened coconut (*nariyal*), shredded, dried
- Water, as needed
- ¾ tsp active dry yeast or 1¼ cups (300 ml) toddy (optional)
- 3–4 Tbsp (37.5–50 g) sugar, divided
- Salt, to taste
- Ghee, for greasing the moulds

• *Method* •

1 In a food processor, combine the soaked rice, uncooked rice, coconut, and a little water or a little toddy (if using). Grind into a thick, smooth paste.

2 If using yeast, in a small bowl stir together ½ cup (120 ml) of warm water and 1 tsp of sugar. Sprinkle the yeast over the water. Set aside for a few minutes to froth.

3 In a large bowl, mix together the rice-coconut paste, remaining sugar, salt to taste, and the yeast mixture or remaining toddy, and enough water to make a thick batter. Cover the bowl and leave to rise, undisturbed, in a warm place for at least 4 hours, or until the batter doubles in volume.

4 Grease small steaming moulds (circular, 2–3-in. deep ramekins) with ghee and pour a little batter into each mould, leaving enough room for it to rise. In a steamer, steam for 10–15 minutes, or until fluffy and cooked through. Serve hot.

SERVES 6

BOLO DE COCO

Baked coconut and semolina cake, popular during Christmas

COOKING TIME
40 MINUTES

• Ingredients •

- 4 Tbsp (60 g) butter, plus more for preparing the cake pan
- 1 cup (200 g) sugar
- ¼ cup (60 ml) water
- 1½ cups plus 1 Tbsp (140 g) unsweetened coconut (*nariyal*), shredded, dried
- 1 cup plus 1 Tbsp (180.5 g) semolina (*suji*)
- ½ tsp vanilla extract
- 1 tsp baking powder
- 3 eggs, separated

• Method •

1 Preheat the oven to 180°C (350°F). Butter a 9-in. round cake pan and set aside.

2 In a saucepan over low heat, combine the sugar and water. Cook until the sugar dissolves completely.

3 Add the coconut. Cook for 2 minutes.

4 Stir in the butter, semolina, and vanilla. Mix well. Remove from the heat and set aside to cool.

5 Once cool, stir in the baking powder.

6 In a small bowl, beat the egg yolks until thick and foamy. Add them to the semolina mixture and stir to combine.

7 In a medium-size bowl, beat the egg whites until stiff. Gently fold into the batter mixture. Pour the batter into the prepared pan and bake for 25–30 minutes until well risen and golden.

8 Remove from the oven and let cool in the pan for 10 minutes. Turn the cake onto a wire rack to cool completely. Cut into pieces and serve.

SERVES 6

KAPPA PURATIYATHU

Tapioca with mustard seeds and coconut

COOKING TIME
25 MINUTES

• Ingredients •

For the tapioca:

- 2 lb, 3 oz (1 kg) fresh tapioca root, peeled, diced
- ½ tsp red chilli powder
- ¼ tsp ground turmeric (*haldi*)
- ½ cup (42.5 g) unsweetened coconut (*nariyal*), grated, dried
- 2 baby onions
- Pinch cumin (*jeera*) seeds
- Salt, to taste

For the tempering:

- 3 Tbsp (45 ml) vegetable oil
- ½ tsp mustard (*rai*) seeds
- 3 Tbsp (30 g) onion, chopped
- 3 sprigs curry leaves (*kadhi patta*), stems removed
- 2 dried red chillies (*sookhi lal mirch*), halved
- 3 Tbsp (30 g) unsweetened coconut (*nariyal*), grated, dried

• Method •

1 **For the tapioca:** In a saucepan, combine the tapioca with enough water to cover. Place it over high heat and boil until tender. Remove from the heat, drain, and set aside to cool. When cool enough to handle, mash the tapioca into a smooth paste.

2 In a small bowl, mix together the red chilli powder and turmeric.

3 In a blender or with a mortar and pestle, crush the coconut, baby onions, and cumin seeds together. Stir in the spice mix.

4 Add this paste to the mashed tapioca. Stir to combine and season to taste with salt. Place the pan over low heat.

5 **For the tempering:** In a wok over low-medium heat, heat the vegetable oil.

6 Add the mustard seeds, onion, curry leaves, dried red chillies, and coconut. Sauté until the ingredients turn brown. Transfer to the tapioca. Mix well and serve hot.

SERVES 4–5

COTTAGE CHEESE SEEKH KEBABS

COOKING TIME
15 MINUTES

Skewered cottage cheese balls

• Ingredients •

- 2 lb, 3 oz (1 kg) cottage cheese (*paneer*), finely grated
- 2 tsp garam masala
- 5 tsp ginger (*adrak*) paste
- 6 green chillies, chopped
- 1 Tbsp (15 ml) lemon (*nimbu*) juice
- ¾ cup (150 g) onions, grated
- 1 tsp red chilli powder
- Salt for seasoning
- 1 tsp white pepper (*safed mirch*) powder
- 4 tsp butter for basting
- 1 Tbsp (7.5 g) cornflour

• Method •

1 Mix all the ingredients, adding the cornflour in the end.

2 Divide this mixture into 15 equal balls.

3 Preheat the oven to 150–175°C (300–350°F).

4 Skewer each ball. Spread by pressing along the length of the skewer with a wet hand, making each kebab about 3–4 in. long, ½ in. apart.

5 Roast in oven / tandoor / charcoal grill for 5–6 minutes. Baste with melted butter and roast for another 2 minutes. Remove from skewers.

6 Garnish with slices of cucumber, tomato, and onion, if desired, and serve hot, accompanied by chutney.

SERVES 2–4

POSTO BORA

Poppy seed patties

COOKING TIME
15 MINIUTES

• Ingredients •

- 2⅔ cups (300 g) poppy seeds (*khus khus*)
- ½ cup (112.5 g) potatoes, boiled, mashed
- ½ cup (60 g) chickpea flour (*besan*)
- 3⅓ Tbsp (30 g) green chillies, chopped
- 2 Tbsp (30 g) onions, chopped
- Salt, to taste
- ½ cup (120 ml) oil

• Method •

1 Soak the poppy seeds in double the quantity of water for 2 hours and keep aside. Grind to a paste.

2 Mix the potatoes with the chickpea flour, green chillies and onions. Add the seasoning and poppy seed paste.

3 Mix all the ingredients together and make 4 balls. Flatten the balls and keep aside.

4 Heat the oil in a pan and shallow-fry the flattened balls till golden brown.

5 Serve hot with tamarind chutney.

SERVES 4

VENDAKKAI PACHADI

Okra in yoghurt

COOKING TIME
15 MINUTES

• *Ingredients* •

- ⅓ cup (100 g) okra (*bhindi*), sliced into thin rounds
- 1 cup (240 g) yoghurt (*dahi*), whisked
- 4 tsp refined oil
- ¼ tsp mustard (*rai*) seeds
- ¾ tsp salt

• *Method* •

1 Heat 3 tsp oil in a pan; fry the okra till it turns golden brown. You can sprinkle a little water and close the pan with a lid.

2 Mix the yoghurt and okra together.

3 Heat the remaining oil; sauté the mustard seeds till they start spluttering.

4 Remove from heat and mix in with the yoghurt mixture. Add salt to taste.

CHEF'S NOTE

This *pachadi* can be served with a variety of dishes including North Indian roti.

SERVES 4–5

TANDOORI COTTAGE CHEESE SALAD

COOKING TIME
15 MINUTES

Roasted, skewered cottage cheese with vegetables and spices

• Ingredients •

- 2 lb, 3 oz (1 kg) cottage cheese (*paneer*)
- 4 tsp capsicum (*Shimla mirch*)
- 4 tsp tomatoes
- 4 tsp onions
- 4 tsp pineapple (*ananas*)
- ½ tsp caraway seeds (*shahi jeera*)
- 1 tsp white pepper (*safed mirch*) powder
- 2 tsp garam masala
- 1 tsp turmeric (*haldi*) powder
- 1 Tbsp (15 ml) lemon (*nimbu*) juice
- Salt, to taste
- ½ cup (120 ml) cream
- ¾ cup (180 g) yoghurt (*dahi*), drained
- 4 Tbsp (30 g) chickpea flour (*besan*) / cornflour
- 2 tsp red chilli powder
- ½ tsp saffron (*kesar*)
- 1 Tbsp (15 g) ginger (*adrak*) paste
- 1 Tbsp (15 g) garlic (*lasan*) paste
- Butter for basting
- 2 tsp chaat masala (optional)

• Method •

1 Wash and cut the cottage cheese, vegetables and pineapple into 1.5-in. cubes.

2 Mix caraway seeds, white pepper, garam masala, turmeric powder, two-thirds of the lemon juice and salt together. Add the cottage cheese cubes to this mixture and refrigerate for 1 hour.

3 Mix together cream, yoghurt and chickpea flour / cornflour. Add remaining ingredients (except butter and chaat masala) and whisk to a fine batter.

4 Add the refrigerated cottage cheese cubes, pineapple cubes and vegetables to the batter and leave to marinate for at least 1 hour.

5 Preheat oven to 150–175°C (300–350°F).

6 Skewer 6 cottage cheese cubes and 4 vegetable-pineapple pieces per skewer (one portion) and pack tightly together.

7 Roast in an oven / tandoor / charcoal grill for 5–6 minutes, basting regularly with melted butter.

8 Sprinkle chaat masala and the remaining lemon juice. Serve hot, garnished with slices of cucumber, tomato and onion, if desired.

CHEF'S NOTE

While making a mixed vegetable salad, cut the tomatoes in vertical slices; they will drip less.

MAKES 12–15

THAIR VADAIS

Spicy dahi vada

COOKING TIME
1 HOUR

• Ingredients •

For the *vadai* (dumplings):
- 2 cups (400 g) split black gram (*dhuli urad dal*), soaked in water overnight, drained
- Salt, to taste
- ½ cup (32 g) curry leaves (*kadhi patta*), chopped
- 2 green chillies, finely chopped
- 1 Tbsp (15 g) fresh ginger (*adrak*), crushed, peeled
- 1 Tbsp (15 ml) freshly squeezed lemon (*nimbu*) juice
- ½ tsp ground asafoetida (*hing*) stirred into ½ cup (120 ml) water

For the spice mix:
- 2 dried red chillies (*sookhi lal mirch*)
- 1 tsp cumin (*jeera*) seeds
- ½ tsp black mustard (*rai*) seeds

For the yoghurt:
- 2 tsp vegetable oil
- ½ cup (32 g) curry leaves (*kadhi patta*), chopped
- 4 green chillies
- 3 cups (720 g) yoghurt (*dahi*)
- 1 cup (240 ml) water
- Salt, to taste
- Vegetable oil, for deep-frying

• Method •

1 **For the *vadai*:** In a blender or food processor, grind the split black gram to a paste. Add salt to taste, the curry leaves, green chillies, ginger, lemon juice, and asafoetida water. Blend into a stiff batter and set aside.

2 **For the spice mix:** In a blender or with a mortar and pestle, coarsely crush the dried red chillies, cumin seeds, and mustard seeds.

3 **For the yoghurt:** In a wok over low-medium heat, heat the vegetable oil.

4 Add the coarsely crushed spice mix, curry leaves, and green chillies. Cook for a few seconds.

5 Stir in the yoghurt and water. Season to taste with salt. Transfer to a bowl and set aside.

6 **To finish the *vadai*:** Clean the wok and return it to the heat. Heat the vegetable oil for deep-frying.

7 Have a bowl of cold water nearby. Gently lower spoonfuls of the black gram batter into the hot oil and deep-fry the *vadais* until golden. Remove and drain on paper towels to remove the excess oil. Transfer the *vadais* to the water for just a few seconds. Remove and gently squeeze out the excess water. Repeat with the remaining batter.

8 Add the *vadais* to the spiced yoghurt and serve cold.

SERVES 2

ARAITHA SAMBHAR

Tangy pigeon peas cooked with vegetables

COOKING TIME
40 MINUTES

• Ingredients •

For the pigeon peas:

- ½ cup (100 g) pigeon peas (*toor dal*), soaked in water for 5 minutes, drained
- 2 cups (480 ml) water
- 4 Tbsp (40 g) Madras onion (pearl onion), chopped
- ½ tsp ground turmeric (*haldi*)
- Salt, to taste
- 1¾ oz (50 g) aubergine (*baigan*), diced
- ½ medium-size green bell pepper, diced
- 1 long drumstick (*saijan ki phalli*), diced
- 1 medium-size potato, diced
- 3 Tbsp (30 g) unsweetened coconut (*nariyal*), grated, dried
- 2 dried red chillies (*sookhi lal mirch*)
- 2½ tsp coriander (*dhaniya*) seeds
- ¾ tsp fenugreek seeds (*methi dana*)
- ½ tsp ground asafoetida (*hing*)
- 2 tsp split Bengal gram (*chana dal*)
- ¾ tsp cumin (*jeera*) seeds
- 2 tsp vegetable oil
- ½ tsp tamarind (*imli*) extract

For the tempering:

- 1 tsp vegetable oil
- ¾ tsp mustard (*rai*) seeds
- ½ tsp cumin (*jeera*) seeds
- ½ tsp aniseed (*saunf*)
- 2 dried red chillies (*sookhi lal mirch*)
- 3 curry leaves (*kadhi patta*)
- Salt, to taste
- 2 Tbsp (2 g) green coriander leaves (*hara dhaniya*), finely chopped

• Method •

1 For the pigeon peas: In a saucepan over high heat, combine the pigeon peas and water and bring to a boil. Cook until tender.

2 Add the onion and turmeric. Season to taste with salt. Continue to cook until everything is soft. Remove the pot from the heat and set aside. Discard the water.

3 In a steamer basket, combine the aubergine, green bell pepper, drumstick, and potato. Steam until soft. Remove and set aside.

4 In a blender or mortar and pestle, grind the coconut, dried red chillies, coriander seeds, fenugreek seeds, asafoetida, split Bengal gram, cumin seeds, and vegetable oil into a smooth paste.

5 Add the steamed vegetables to the pigeon pea mix. Stir to combine, place the pan over low heat, and cook for 10–12 minutes.

6 Stir in the ground paste and tamarind extract. Cook for 5 minutes more.

7 For the tempering: In a wok over medium-high heat, heat the vegetable oil.

8 Add the mustard seeds, cumin seeds, aniseed, dried red chillies, and curry leaves. Sauté until the seeds begin to crackle and the curry leaves turn crisp. Pour the tempering into the pigeon peas and mix well. Season to taste with salt. Serve hot, garnished with coriander.

SERVES 4

VELLARIKKAI PACHADI

Cucumber in yoghurt

COOKING TIME
3 MINUTES

• Ingredients •

- 1 medium-size cucumber, grated
- 1 cup (240 g) yoghurt (*dahi*), whisked till smooth
- ½ tsp refined oil ¼ tsp mustard (*rai*) seeds
- Salt, to taste
- A few sprigs green coriander (*hara dhaniya*), chopped

• Method •

1 Heat the oil in a pan; sauté the mustard seeds till they start spluttering.

2 Combine all the ingredients.

CHEF'S NOTE

It is best to keep all the ingredients ready and combine them just before serving.